A Century of FIESTA In San Antonio

Court of Venice, 1965.

— *Billo Smith*

A Century of FIESTA In _____ San Antonio

by Jack Maguire

In Cooperation with

Fiesta San Antonio Commission, Inc.

EAKIN PRESS ★ Austin, Texas

FIRST EDITION

Copyright © 1990
By Jack Maguire

Published in the United States of America
By Eakin Press, P.O. Drawer 90159, Austin, Texas 78709-0159

ALL RIGHTS RESERVED. No part of this book may be reproduced in any form without written permission from the publisher, except for brief passages included in a review appearing in a newspaper or magazine.

Library of Congress Cataloging-in-Publication Data

Maguire, Jack, 1919–
    A century of fiesta in San Antonio / by Jack Maguire : in cooperation with the Fiesta San Antonio Commission, Inc.
        p.   cm.
    Includes index.
    ISBN 0-89015-793-6 (hardback) : $24.95
    1. Fiesta San Antonio, San Antonio, Texas. 2. San Antonio (Tex.) — Social life and customs. I. Fiesta San Antonio Commission. II. Title.
GT4811.S25M34   1990
394.2′69764351--dc20
                                                                                    90-44619
                                                                                    CIP

Cover photo by Al Rendon

For Ann, my Queen,
who makes life a perpetual Fiesta.

Contents

Preface

Fiesta is the psalm of San Antonio — a hymn sung for a century now by the citizenry to glorify the conviction that theirs is a place of halcyonic sophistication on the one hand and an impregnable refuge against the soul-wearying onslaught of day-to-day living on the other.

San Antonio, like some people, has a way of endearing itself to all. To Texans it is the place of our roots, the Mecca to which every Texan journeys at one time or another to restore the soul. And each April since 1891, Fiesta has provided a kind of holy week when the faithful gather to celebrate and relive the past that has made this place truly one of the nation's unique cities.

Just as there is no other place quite like San Antonio, there is not another event anywhere quite like Fiesta. It was the idea of a tourist from Chicago who thought the city of the Alamo should do something to memorialize the heroes who died in defense of that shrine. An alert woman took on the project as a mission of the town's socially elite. The original sponsors came largely from two groups: wealthy families from the Old South and aristocratic German immigrants. They had come by choice to this Spanish/Mexican settlement, a place that was a thriving Indian village when Columbus discovered America.

These newcomers wanted to build a cultural oasis in the brush country of Texas. They succeeded.

They called that first major effort in 1891 the Battle of Flowers. It was hardly an extravaganza, but it was the beginning of a tradition that has grown into the Fiesta of today. In the century since, large numbers of Chinese, Czechs, French, Greeks, Lebanese, Poles, and a dozen other nationalities have joined them. Each has added a new and exciting dimension to the event.

This is their story.

Acknowledgments

This book represents the combined work of many.

My special thanks to Mrs. Joanna Parrish, the coordinator of Fiesta Centennial. To produce such a book was the idea of the Long-Range Planning Committee of the Fiesta Commission — a group made up of former presidents. A written history was the first project decided upon for the Centennial, and I am grateful to each member. It was a special pleasure to work with Mrs. Parrish in every phase of the research. Without her help, this book could not have been written.

Tom Shelton, my friend and associate when I was executive director of the Institute of Texan Cultures, and Carol Canty, a Fiesta Commission volunteer, spent days finding and identifying most of the photographs used in this book. Agnes Harwood, another commission volunteer, loaned me her scrapbooks on past Fiestas and helped me substantiate many of the facts needed.

Charles Kilpatrick, publisher of the *San Antonio Express/News*, and George Irish, publisher of the *San Antonio Light*, generously granted permission for carte blanche use of historic photos from the collections of both newspapers now a part of the Institute of Texan Cultures Library.

Special thanks is due Marianna Jones and Nellie Weincek of the San Antonio Conservation Society for their help in producing facts and photographs. Generous help also came from Santiego Escobedo of the Daughters of the Republic of Texas Library at the Alamo and the San Antonio Museum Association. Both institutions made their extensive photo collections available.

I am especially grateful to Ike S. Kampmann, Jr., grandson of the president of the first Battle of Flowers and nephew of the first Queen selected by the Order of the Alamo. Mr. Kampmann provided me not only with a great deal of biographical information about his illustrious family, but also the photographs of the Kampmann ladies used in the book.

Lee Kelly, columnist for the *Austin American-Statesman* and an old friend, helped when we needed it most. When we were unable to locate a photograph of Miss Ida Archer, the first Fiesta Queen, Lee ran an item in her column asking for help. Before the end of the day, the Austin History Center had telephoned that it had available the photo that appears in the book. We are especially grateful to that fascinating repository of Austin history.

Carol Canty, Marshall Clegg, Eugene S. Carrington, Agnes Harwood, Vivian Hamlin Terrett, Henry and Mary Ann Noonan Guerra, Bill and Joanna Parrish, and Inell Schooler (1990 Fiesta Commission president) all took the time to read, edit, and make suggestions regarding the manuscript. Marleen Pedroza, executive vice-president of the commission, and her staff were helpful in myriad ways.

To each of the above, and the many others not named who assisted in so many ways, my sincere thanks and appreciation.

San Antonio, which has such a special place in my own heart, also deserves some thanks. I attended my first Fiesta in 1936 and have missed few since. The ten years that I called that city home, and was actively involved in Fiesta events, were among the best and happiest of my life. San Antonio is, and always shall be, my second home.

Perhaps I am most indebted to my wife, Ann, a fine writer, researcher, and editor. She was involved in every phase of this work and deserves credit as the co-author.

JACK MAGUIRE
Fredericksburg, Texas
October 1990

1

An Idea That Became a Tradition

"Life is a festival only to the wise."
— *Ralph Waldo Emerson*

It all began in the spring of 1891 with the idea of a tourist from Chicago. It was never intended to be anything more than a flower festival commemorating the Battle of San Jacinto and the end of Texas' successful revolt against Mexico. That it was given impetus by the unexpected visit of a short, bearded, and rather unimposing visitor from Washington was pure coincidence. The latter visitor was proud of the fact that he was both a Presbyterian elder and Sunday school teacher. He also happened to be the twenty-third president of the United States.

While the planned trip of Benjamin Harrison to San Antonio was *raison détre* for a salute of some magnitude (no White House occupant had come calling before), the festival had not been planned for him. Weeks before the announcement from Washington that the president would trek to Texas, W. J. Ballard, vacationing in San Antonio from his Chicago base, had suggested the notion of an April celebration.

The Real Battle That Started It All

At the time, neither Ballard nor anyone else was aware that the nation's chief executive was planning a visit to San Antonio on April 20. The following day marked a very special event in Texas history and had been selected as the date for the flower festival.

On April 21, 1836, at San Jacinto, a plain that lies not far from today's Lyndon Baines Johnson Space Center, the Texian Army under Gen. Sam Houston had routed Gen. Antonio Lopez de Santa Anna's forces and made Texas forever independent of Mexican rule. San Jacinto was the kind of battle history never forgets. It pitted a ragtag group of vol-

unteers armed only with muskets, rifles, and two tiny cannon against a much larger, well-trained, and superbly equipped army. Although the odds were overwhelming, the Texians knew that by winning this last battle they could revenge the Alamo. Less than two months earlier, Santa Anna had devastated the old San Antonio mission, killing all of the 189 defenders.

Houston, who was at Gonzales with 1,400 troops when the Alamo fell, began a retreat. By the time he reached San Jacinto — the farthest point that he could go — his force had dwindled to about 800. General Santa Anna, with his much larger force, was camped nearby. All chance of escape had been cut off for both armies and a showdown was inevitable.

At 4:30 P.M. on April 21, the Mexicans were at *siesta* as their commander reportedly dallied with a beautiful mulatto girl in his tent. Houston decided to attack. Only eighteen minutes later, 630 Mexicans were dead and 730 others (including Santa Anna) were prisoners. The Alamo had been revenged, and the Texas revolt against Mexico had triumphed. The Texians lost only ten men.

Three Good Reasons for a Fiesta

The Battle of San Jacinto, to the visiting Ballard, was such a significant day in Texas history that it deserved special recognition. He also pointed out that two centuries earlier, on June 13, 1691, an expedition under Domingo de Teran, the first Spanish governor of the province of Texas, had approached a river the Indians called Yanaguana. Teran's priest, Father Damian Masanet, named the spot San Antonio de Padua.

Above: Honoring the Alamo heroes and those of San Jacinto always has been the principal purpose of Fiesta San Antonio. A pilgrimage to the Alamo shrine is still an annual event sponsored by the Daughters of the Republic of Texas.

— San Antonio Express/News
Collection, Institute of Texan Cultures

Below: Ethnic celebrations have been a part of San Antonio's history since it began as an Indian settlement called Yanaguana in the seventeenth century. They remain an important part of the city's life, as this float from a Battle of Flowers Parade in the 1930s indicates.

— *San Antonio Museum Association*

This meant that 1891 was both the bicentennial of St. Anthony's town as well as the fifty-fifth anniversary of San Jacinto — surely good reasons for a giant celebration. Since the event was inspired by two important historical dates, Ballard suggested that it also commemorate still another — the fall of the Alamo.

In suggesting such an idea to his friends in San Antonio, Ballard knew it would get a hearing. Then, as now, the city of the Alamo was unlike any other. And its residents had never rejected taking on another celebration.

In the almost 200 years since the arrival of the first Europeans at a site believed to be near where Loop 410 South crosses the river, San Antonio had become a bustling city. The metamorphosis of the one-time Indian village, mission site, and presidio into an important town had really begun on March 9, 1731. On that day, fifteen families from the Canary Islands arrived, sent by the king of Spain to colonize what had been only a mission and a military outpost. A townsite was laid out for them, a governing council was appointed, and Texas had its first organized municipal government. The new arrivals also had inadvertently planted the seeds of Fiesta.

Music was one. Except for Indian drums and chants, the only form of music heard in Texas before the arrival of the islanders was the hymn. That form was introduced by Spanish *padres* in the missions they established. However, when these first Spanish colonists arrived, a marching band was among the military contingent sent to protect them. Included with their cattle and household goods were guitars, castanets, and other instruments, and soon they were holding *musicales* on Main Plaza. These may not have been memorable, but they were the forerunners of the extravaganzas of marching bands, symphonies, country/western hoedowns, and *conjunto* that orchestrate today's Fiesta San Antonio.

Yes, There Were Nobles in Old San Antonio

The second seed planted by the Canary Islanders was that of nobility. By stretching the imagination, Fiesta's custom of crowning its own royalty can be traced to the fact that true nobles once lived here. Although the Canary Island colonists were commoners who espoused equality, an old custom of their country made them, as first arrivals in a new colony, nobles of the realm. Thus the heads of the fifteen families were automatically given the lowest rank among the nobility — that of *hijo hidalgo*, literally "noble son." It was a rank equivalent to knighthood in England.

Whereas *hidalgo* was a title for life that could be passed to descendants, Kings and Queens of Fiesta hold their royal titles only for a year. And unlike San Antonio's first nobles, the responsibilities of these modern royalists are both brief and purely ceremonial. Not so with the *hidalgos*. By order of their new king, they had to plan and carry out themselves an event that might be termed the first authentic Fiesta in the city's history. It preceded the current fete by 144 years.

This was a weeklong revel that began on January 27, 1747, to celebrate the coronation of Ferdinand VI. He had ascended the Spanish throne the previous August but had delayed the observance of his new status for five months to give the colonists time to prepare a proper festival. (By today's standards, that timetable was too short. Now planners of Fiesta San Antonio begin work on the next year's event within hours after their current one ends.)

The First Battle of Flowers?

The *hidalgos* of San Antonio de Bexar, however, worked fast. With help from the 200-plus soldiers at the presidio, they built a four-story replica of a royal castle on Market Plaza. It was the background for mock battles staged to depict how Spain had won its independence from Moorish domination. It also was the site for concerts, dances, and political speeches.

Although Fiesta San Antonio uses parade floats instead of castles to make its point, there are parallels between that celebration almost 250 years ago and the one today. Just as Fiesta San Antonio always opens with a ceremony at the Alamo, the celebration in 1747 began with an assembly at the Spanish Governor's Palace. The royal decree proclaiming the crowning of the new monarch was read, there were speeches by the governor and other notables, and then the entire community went to the San Fernando Church for Mass.

Once these solemn rites ended, entertainment was the talisman for the next week. Although there were not nearly as many nor such a variety of goodies as are available at the modern Fiesta's "Night in Old San Antonio," there were food vendor stands along Main and Military plazas. And there were constant *mascaradas*: parades of costumed marchers wearing masks. There were even night *mascaradas* with the participants carrying lighted torches in the

Long before the first
Battle of Flowers, San
Antonio had a reputation
as a city of the arts. By
the late 1870s, the city
had museums and thea-
ters good enough to at-
tract the likes of Edwin
Booth and others. Lillie
Langtry, famed for her
music hall performances
as "The Jersey Lily,"
was among them.
— *Institute of Texan Cultures*

Carriages, providing they were decorated, were welcome additions to early Fiesta parades.
— *San Antonio Museum Association*

manner of today's Fiesta Flambeau Parade.

Since this first display of merriment and joviality in the embryonic settlement of San Antonio de Bexar two and a half centuries ago, *fiesta* (as the Spanish called these diversions) has changed. But not much. So has the city, but not much.

By 1890, when the first modern Fiesta was planned, San Antonio had grown from the village of about 1,000 (including Mission Indians) that it had been in 1747 to a thriving trade center of 38,000. It had not, however, been so busy developing into a city that it had forgotten to dedicate much of its time and resources to conviviality.

There's a Fiesta Every Week

Secular and religious holidays were always a source of diversion and jollity. It was, and is, a town where public feasts and ceremonies are almost a daily part of community life. Before Texas won its own freedom, Mexican Independence Day *(Diez y Seis de Septiembre)* was one of the big holidays that called for extraordinary celebrations.

Although limited to one or two days, some of these events were not unlike those of today's Fiesta. On the night before the holiday, hundreds would gather to parade through the streets to announce

Ethnic celebrations have always been an integral part of
San Antonio life and predated the first Battle of Flowers
by many years. This photograph of a Diez y Seis (Mexican Independence Day) observance was made in the
1880s.

         — *Catholic Archives, Austin*

Floats in early Battle of Flowers parades were decorated wagons drawn by horses and frequently adorned with pretty women.

— *Institute of Texan Cultures*

the next day's festivities by ringing bells, firing pistols, and playing music. On the holiday itself, there would be another parade, political speeches, and dances and picnics.

San Antonio was a special place even then. Its growth had been spurred by the cattle empires that spread from Alamo Plaza for hundreds of miles to the south and west. Ranching had turned the once sleepy village into a commercial center whose large stockyards and three railroads provided distribution to every part of the U.S. But unlike the other "cow towns" that sprang up in the South and West following the Civil War, it was like two communities in one. While it was a favorite of ranch hands

for a hundred miles around as the place to gather to drink, gamble, and patronize the several houses of prostitution, it also was a cultural oasis on the edge of the rugged Texas brush country.

"Viva la Difference!"

Its polyglot population was one reason San Antonio was "different." From the arrival of the first Europeans, San Antonio's citizenry has been a diverse sampling of many ethnic groups. In 1891 at least a fifth of the entire populace were aristocratic Germans. Of the almost equal number of Americans, English, and Irish, many were second-gener-

Since the 1700s, San Antonio's beautiful plazas have been the scenes of celebrations. Alamo Plaza is no exception. In 1910, Fiesta was called Spring Carnival. As a part of the entertainment, a professional traveling carnival operated on Alamo Plaza in front of the post office.

— Ann Russell Collection,
Institute of Texan Cultures

tion Southerners from old, well-to-do families. From the beginning, Indians, and later Mexicans, had made up the largest segment of the citizenry, and there also were growing neighborhoods of French, Polish, Italian, Spanish, and Chinese people. It was a trilingual town, with English, German, and Spanish the common languages.

Because each of these groups contributed much of their own culture to the lifestyle of the community, San Antonio was considered unique. While Dallas, Houston, and even Austin tried separately to achieve a degree of sophistication, San Antonio was already building a reputation in Texas and in the nation as a community like no other.

Unlike most former frontier communities, its cultural roots are deep. As early as 1851, Catholic nuns from France had established Ursuline, a first-

rate academy for girls. The Brothers of Mary, also from France, opened a boys' school — St. Mary's. These and the later German private schools were considered models for the nation. By 1885, a thriving business college was in operation. However, interests in culture extended beyond education.

In 1853 the Germans had organized their first exclusive social club, the Casino Association. Another of their first projects was an opera house. Not to be outdone, the wealthy Southern Anglos formed the San Antonio Club, still one of the city's most exclusive dining and watering places. The city's attraction to visitors was enhanced in 1859 when William Menger built on Alamo Plaza what was described as the "finest hotel between New Orleans and San Francisco."

In 1920 members of the San Antonio Music Club decorated this automobile with a statue of Cupid and covered the car with fresh flowers.

— *San Antonio Museum Association*

A City of the Arts

Recognizing San Antonio's importance in international trade, Mexico had opened its first consulate there in 1879. A Museum of Natural History was operating, and the town had sponsored the San Antonio International Exposition, one of the nation's first successful world fairs. Actors like Edwin Booth and Joseph Jefferson appeared on local stages, and musicals ranging from opera to German *sangerfests* were regular fare. When famed actress Sarah Bernhardt stopped there in 1887, she called San Antonio "the art center of Texas."

With all of this, plus gas lights, electric streetcars, artesian wells, and beautiful San Pedro Park, San Antonio was not the rough frontier village on the edge of the Texas brush country that most outlanders believed it to be. Thus it is hardly surprising that to W. J. Ballard, the vacationer from Chicago, the city seemed the perfect environment for a special kind of celebration. His concept that the event memorialize the Alamo and San Jacinto heroes while celebrating the city's bicentennial and honoring Texas independence would give the occasion enduring significance.

From the first, Ballard's plan gained the broad support expected from a community that has staged shows of one kind or another throughout its recorded history. It is said that friendly Indians showed up in their feathers and war paint and danced during Father Masanet's Mass dedicating San Antonio de Padua on that June day in 1691. When the Canary Island *hidalgos* came forty years later, they brought along with their noble titles and

For many years, Fiesta Queens rode on horse-drawn
floats and were accompanied by a retinue of mounted
aides. This is Queen Josephine Woodhull of the Court of
the Year in 1915.

Although San Antonians have always loved parades, they sometimes like to poke fun at them. In the early 1900s, "burlesque parades" like this one were staged along with Battle of Flowers events. Entries took pot shots at everything from the Fiesta royalty, as here, to local political figures and celebrities.

— *San Antonio Museum Association*

guitars the custom of singing Christmas carols and producing the pageants "Los Pastores" and "Las Posadas." After more than 250 years, these are still reenacted each year at Yuletide in San Antonio.

Acrobats and Tamale Queens

This early fascination for music, drama, and merrymaking never lessened. In 1807, Lt. Zebulon Pike of the U.S. Army visited the Villa de Bejar, a village of some 2,000 souls. He wrote that it was home to companies of acrobats, clowns, and tumblers. In the 1840s, William Bollaert, a writer and geographer sent to Texas at the behest of the British government, recalled that he was entertained in the streets by a company that included a clown, rope dancing, tumblers, and short farcical comedies. The enjoyment of the spectators was enhanced by booths vending whiskey and chili queens selling *tamales calientes* on the fringes of the crowd.

A decade later, Frederick Law Olmsted, a correspondent for the *New York Times*, wrote in his 1857 book, *Journey Through Texas*, how "a permanent company of Mexican mountebanks" dressed in spangled tights performed two or three times a week in San Antonio's plazas. Their nighttime shows, illuminated by torches, were accented with drums and tambourines.

Long before today's Fiesta was born, the two elite social groups in town — the German immigrants who made their fortunes in business and banking and upper-class newcomers from the Old South — had held their own celebrations. The genteel Southerners, joined by the increasing numbers of French families in old San Antonio, had replicated events like New Orleans' Mardi Gras, but on a smaller scale. For at least forty years, the Germans had staged street marches commemorating holidays in their Fatherland. Beginning in the 1880s, this ethnic group had sponsored an annual Volk Fest that brought thousands of their countrymen to San Antonio from across Texas. There were parades, band concerts, picnics of German food, gymnastics by the *Turnverein,* speeches, *sangerfests,* and fireworks.

San Antonio: Every Texan's Second Home

Even if such events had not been an integral part of daily life from the beginning, San Antonio still would have been a magnet that draws more visitors than any other spot in Texas. Its historic Alamo has been bringing people from around the world for more than a century. Others come to admire homes built forty years and more before the American Revolution. And what other city has blended for so long and so harmoniously such a variety of ethnic groups? No wonder, as the late, great folklorist J. Frank Dobie wrote: "Every Texan has two homes — his own and San Antonio."

Thus the celebration suggested in 1891 was only the continuation of a long tradition of events designed to acquaint others with the friendliness of Texans fortunate enough to live in their state's most charming city. The decision to take action on the plan became compelling, however, when positive word came that President Harrison would, indeed, arrive aboard a special train on April 20.

The first flower festival was on its way.

San Antonio always has been a city of street food vendors. This busy tamale stand was on the south side of Military Plaza in the 1880s. Much later, women vendors called "chili queens" operated dozens of stands around the plazas until health regulations closed them about the time of World War II.

— *Institute of Texan Cultures*

2

The First Battle of Flowers

"What a desolate place would be a world without flowers!
It would be a face without a smile; a feast without a welcome."
— **Clara Lucas Balfour** (1808–1878)

In the days before helicopters and jets made the occupant of the nation's highest office almost a commuter to every part of the world, presidents spent far more time at the White House than they did on the road. When they did travel, Texas had never been in their itinerary. Of the thirteen who had held the office since 1845, when Texas joined the Union, not one had visited the state in the ensuing forty-six years. Even James K. Polk, who had advocated the annexation of Texas over strong opposition, never got around to visiting the place. Zachary Taylor and Ulysses S. Grant had been stationed in Texas as soldiers, but never expressed any interest in returning after becoming president.

It was enough to give any proud Texan — and they all are — an inferiority complex.

When Benjamin Harrison announced that he wanted to be the first president to pay an official call on the Lone Star State, it was no wonder that the news was met with excitement from the Red River to the Rio Grande. Even San Antonians, who for more than two centuries had hosted Spanish viceroys, great generals, poets, and the famous and infamous from all over, were overjoyed that Harrison was coming.

Since plans for the first Battle of Flowers already were in the making when word of his trip came, the event never was intended as a special salute to the president. His visit was regarded only as an extra added attraction. The Battle was, as Fiesta today continues to be, the city's way of paying homage to the Alamo dead and the heroes of San Jacinto. The only concession the planners made to the presidential visit was to stage their event on April 20. On April 21, the hallowed anniversary of San Jacinto, President Harrison's special train would be

rolling through the West Texas brush country.

Ballard's idea to stage such a fete had won the quick acceptance that he expected from the community. The newspapers supported it with editorials, mass meetings of citizens approved it, and it became the pet project of a relative newcomer to San Antonio, Mrs. James Luther Slayden.

Ellen Maury Slayden had come to the city as a bride. A Virginia-born aristocrat, she was one of many well-to-do Southern immigrants who, with the large coterie of German settlers, made up San Antonio's social elite. On her first visit to Texas, Ellen had fallen in love with both the state and James Luther Slayden, a rancher and cotton broker. They were married in 1883. San Antonio became their permanent home, except for periods in later years when they spent some time in Washington after his election to Congress.

How the French Inspired a Mexican Fiesta

Once Ellen Slayden had decided to see Ballard's idea through, she enlisted another relative newcomer, Mrs. J. S. Alexander, in the enterprise. The latter's husband, president of Texas National Bank, became an immediate ally of the ladies. Alexander, a native of Philadelphia, had received part of his education in Europe and had been a banker in London before coming to Texas. It was he who would suggest the form the first Fiesta would take.

While discussing ideas for the affair, Alexander mentioned that he had been impressed by a flower parade that he had seen while living in Europe. Nice, France, the Queen City of the Cote d'Azur, had the same interests as San Antonio in attracting more tourists. In 1873 it had started a Carnival

Babies had their own parade in early Fiestas. Held in Travis Park across from the St. Anthony Hotel, these parades were an added attraction preceding the Battle of Flowers. Roy Thompson is shown in the 1906 parade.

— Battle of Flowers Association

Week to advertise its flower market, and the high-light of the celebration was a battle between beautiful women using blossoms as ammunition. He had attended one of the "fights" and thought it might be adapted for the amusement of San Antonians and the visitors they hoped to lure.

When Mrs. Slayden recalled that she had seen a similar event in Spain and someone else had watched a flower battle in Mexico, the theme was unanimously adopted. It was at this point that Alexander and Col. H. B. Andrews, a prominent rancher and president of the prestigious San Antonio Club, quietly mentioned that the women might find some male help useful. They also suggested that the planning committee be expanded to include wives of some of the other members of the club, since they represented the city's best society.

Winning Friends and Influencing Men

When the women agreed, Colonel Andrews invited them to meet at the club's headquarters. So it was that the entire committee descended on the off-limits-to-women precincts of that male bastion where Andrews himself spoke in their behalf.

"The startled gentlemen, who up to this time had not had a woman at one of their meetings, listened with interest," Mary Etta McGimsey later would relate in her book, *A History of the Battle of Flowers Association*.

The men did more than listen. They responded by naming a committee of their own to assist with plans for the project. Most important of all, they agreed to raise the necessary funds to inaugurate it.

Although the celebration had been first suggested by a man, its theme provided by another, and the funds for its start made possible by a men's club, it was, and still is, a women's project. To make sure that it remained so, the women organized the all-female group to be known forever after as the Battle of Flowers Association.

Apparently, it was assumed that Ellen Slayden, who had started the idea toward reality, would be named to head the organization. At the first meeting, however, the members chose Mrs. H. D. Kampmann as their chairman.

Elizabeth Kampmann was an ideal choice. She was a native of San Antonio, a descendant of one of the first families, and the wife of a prominent banker. In the same year that she was chosen to lead the Battle of Flowers, her husband had bought the Menger Hotel, then as now one of the most famous inns in the U.S. Also she, with Ellen Slayden

and Mrs. Alexander, had been a principal architect in planning the project.

First "Battle" Faced Ammunition Shortage

It was decided early on that San Antonio would not try to compete in scope with the similar events in Nice and Cannes. This was Texas, not France, and a city where the Spanish tradition of *fiesta* already was well established. Also, it was a place where a wealth of wild and garden flowers was always available in April. Their "battle of the flowers" would make use of these native blooms.

Getting the show ready called for a race with the clock. The first real planning session wasn't held until April 13, only seven days before President Harrison was to arrive. Because heavy rains had played havoc with local gardens, the supply of flowers appeared to be far short of the blossoms needed to decorate twelve carriages and innumerable bicycles, as well as provide camouflage for the children who were to be dressed to look like real flowers. An SOS went out to Beeville, Victoria, and other nearby communities for help. Gardens there had escaped the rains, and citizens responded to San Antonio's needs by rushing in flowers by train.

Much discussion was devoted to the handling of the "ammunition" to be used in the battle. The committee ruled that only small nosegays, a single rose, and no more than two of any other flowers could be tossed in the attack. Large bouquets were considered dangerous.

In addition to the carriages, a call was sent out for bicyclists to adorn their wheels with blossoms and foliage and join the cavalcade. (A local bicycling club had just been formed and riding the two-wheelers had become a popular sport with both young men and women.) One float would carry the children dressed as flowers.

"There will also be another float," the *Daily Express* reported, "of young girls whose ages do not permit them to be called children, while at the same time they cannot be classed as young ladies!" Bringing up the rear would be a brigade of Shetland ponies appropriately adorned. Perhaps the most unusual parade entry, and a predecessor of the elaborate theme floats of modern Fiesta parades, would replicate "The Little Old Woman Who Lived in a Shoe."

Although the ladies planned each detail of the event, they shirked the responsibility of deciding which entries deserved prizes. They handed that assignment to a panel of male judges.

Flower-bedecked bicycles were an important part of the first parade.
— *Daughters of the Republic of Texas Alamo Library*

Over the years, Fiesta has offered a variety of entertainment. In this 1955 photo, aerialists perform on a tight-wire high above the Alamo.
— San Antonio Express/News *Collection, Institute of Texan Cultures*

Rain On Their Parade

By Monday morning, April 20, 1891, everything except the weather was in readiness. At exactly 9:15, the five-car special train carrying President Harrison and his party arrived at the Southern Pacific station (known then as the Sunset Depot). Arriving along with the distinguished visitors, however, was a continuation of the downpour that had plagued the city for days. Despite the disappointment of the ladies and their famous guests, the flower battle had to be postponed. Hoping the weather would improve, the new date was set for the following Friday. By then, of course, President Harrison would be long gone from Texas.

Neither the rain nor the postponement of the Battle of Flowers dampened the warm reception for the president, however. Armed with umbrellas, a committee of prominent couples was on hand to welcome the short-statured, long-whiskered Harrison for a pleasant three-hour stay. Most of those greeting the Republican president were Democrats, but politics were laid aside during the visit except for a few humorous jibes from partisans of both parties. Wisely, the president had invited a Democrat, popular Governor James Stephen Hogg, to ride in his special train. It was a gesture that immediately endeared him to his Texas hosts.

Because of the weather, the San Antonio women stayed aboard the train with Mrs. Harrison while the men formed a procession of carriages to give the president the equivalent of a modern Gray Line tour around town. The plan was to take the chief executive by the Alamo, then to Fort Sam Houston, and finally to the Opera House.

Harrison, a brigadier general in the Civil War (remembered for leading his regiment in prayer as well as in action), especially wanted to visit this fort

By 1917, the world was about to war and the automobile was fast replacing the horse. This entry in the Civic and Trades Display Parade that year demonstrated the latest model of the successor to the old delivery wagon.

— Institute of Texan Cultures

Ellen Maury Slayden took the idea of a Chicago visitor in 1891 and turned it into a celebration that has continued for a century.

— *Battle of Flowers Association*

now that he was commander-in-chief. Again the deluge of rain caused a schedule change, and the official party was driven first to what had been planned as the climactic stop — the Grand Opera House on Alamo Plaza.

Since the president's schedule had been announced in the papers the day before, only a handful had gathered at the Opera House because the official party was not due there until 11:00 A.M. Word of the change soon got around, however, and within minutes the place was packed. The next day, the *San Antonio Daily Express* reported it this way:

"In the history of a house that has contained vast crowds on many notable occasions, there was

never anything seen to approach the multitudes within its doors yesterday. Every seat, every box, every passage and inch of standing room was filled. The audience was gathered together in a solid mass, but no one thought of discomfort."

Texas: "Where God Reigns and Intelligence Is Great"

President Harrison obviously was pleased by the size of the reception and he responded with a smile to one unique greeting. Hanging from the rail of the upper balcony and facing the Opera House stage was a huge banner with these words:

THE LONE STAR STATE
THE MORNING STAR OF FREEDOM,
RIVALLED ONLY BY
THE ASCENDING SUN OF THE NATION

Although suffering from laryngitis and apologizing for his voice, the president responded with a Texas brag of his own.

"The great capabilities, industrial development, climate and variety of productions give prominence for Texas among the greatest states of the Union. Wealth and commerce are timid and still only come where God reigns and intelligence is great!"

Despite the weather and his sore throat, the president had not lost his sense of humor.

"I assure you that I sympathize with you in that the day is so unpropitious, yet I have been told that this rain is worth $5 million to you. This being the case, our regrets are modified. I doubtless am the cause of this downpour, and if it is really worth that much of Texas, I will not ask for more than half."

It probably is true that the rains that deluged the first visit of a president to San Antonio were worth $5 million to the ranchers and farmers. But that first Battle of Flowers, which the weather forced President Harrison to miss, was also an historic first which has been worth many times $5 million in the century since. It was staged exactly as planned four days after the president's visit. Despite Harrison's absence, planners were so confident of its success that they passed a resolution calling for it to be an annual event on the city's social calendar. It has been each year since.

3

The Ladies in Yellow

"There is a woman at the beginning of all great things."
— **Alphonse de Lamartine,** French poet (1790–1869)

Until the ladies staged their Battle of Flowers, San Antonio had always had the reputation of being a male domain. No more.

Today the 400 women of "The Light Brigade," as they are sometimes called, bear some of the most prominent names in San Antonio. They are seen everywhere, wearing wide-brimmed yellow straw hats and dresses that range from mustard yellow to saffron and daffodil, with a kaleidoscope of hues in between. Yellow identifies them as members of the exclusive Battle of Flowers Association, the organization that started Fiesta San Antonio a century ago, when they appear at events sponsored by their organization.

That a handful of women could develop what they intended only as one parade into an annual ten-day event attracting hundreds of thousands of local residents and visitors alike seemed an impossible task in the San Antonio of 1891. Since the village of San Antonio de Bexar began in 1691, women had been in the minority.

Except for Indian squaws, the personnel involved in the early missions were all men. Family life didn't begin until the arrival of the Canary Islanders in 1731. As the settlement became more important as a military base, many of the soldiers brought along their wives. Even after the Civil War, however, when ranching began on a large scale and San Antonio became the "cowmen's capital," the ladies were given little prominence in community affairs unless they were social.

Thus many of the cattle barons and businessmen of 1891 were astounded when a group of their wives decided to present before all comers the event they named "the Battle of Flowers." The ladies

were, after all, the town's social elite, descended mostly from the aristocracy of the Old South. They were talented, knowledgeable, and intelligent, but their traditional role required only that they be good homemakers and carry out the expected social proprieties. That they would venture outside the home to plan and execute a public spectacle, even for the most worthy patriotic cause, was a concern to many males.

Fortunately, there were other men who applauded and supported the idea, as related earlier. Once the first Battle of Flowers was planned, other males helped. Through the years since, men have continued to be involved when called upon. The organization, however, remains an exclusive association of women.

What's in a Name?

Early on, the members had named their organization and the event they would sponsor "The Battle of Flowers." The name served a double purpose: It aptly described the friendly flower-tossing feature of the parade and it also was a manner of memorializing the fall of the Alamo and the heroes of San Jacinto. Finding a generic term to describe their "Battle of Flowers" was more difficult.

Because of its serious purpose, the event was more than an ordinary parade. Its sponsors wanted it to be festive and fun. However, they wanted it to inspire reflection on the past, especially on the successful revolt against Mexico. Most of all, they wanted it to reflect the city's heritage.

"Carnival" was one name considered, but it was discarded because its origin was French. Since

Fiesta always attracts celebrities ranging from First
Ladies of the United States to Hollywood stars. Here
comedian Red Skelton makes a serious speech at the
solemn pilgrimage to the Alamo sponsored by the
Daughters of the Republic of Texas.

— *Joe Elicson Collection, DRT Library at the Alamo*

the *padres* who discovered this area and selected it as a site for a mission were Spanish, the name should somehow relate to that ethnic group. *Fiesta* was a Spanish word for a celebration honoring a saint, and this event was to be in a place named for St. Anthony. So Fiesta it would be, although the people called it "carnival" for the first years of its existence.

By whatever name, the 1891 celebration, under the leadership of Eda Kampmann, was more of a social happening than an amusement for the masses. All citizens were invited to the Battle of Flowers and most of them accepted. However, it was primarily the wives of San Antonio Club members, their friends and neighbors, plus descendants of veterans of the Texas revolution who were active participants.

This first "carnival" was such an anticipated success that it was decided, even before the first carriages rolled around Alamo Plaza in April 1891, to repeat it in 1892. For the second celebration, members replaced the chairman with a president and named Mrs. J. J. Stevens to that office. Men were excluded from membership.

Today the Battle of Flowers Association is the only all-woman organization in the world that plans and stages a major parade in its entirety, and has for 100 years, and they do so without any paid clerical help. However, after the first ten years of doing everything connected with the celebration themselves (except fund-raising), they agreed that the time had come to share the responsibilities.

"Give Me Men, Stout-Hearted Men"

In 1901 they decided to limit their involvement primarily to the growing social activities attendant on the event and leave the financing and coordination to others. Having learned at the beginning that they needed men to help raise funds, they did the unexpected and elected a male as president, Ben Hammond. He was so successful that L. J. Hart was picked to succeed him in 1902, followed by H. E. Hildebrand in 1903. It appeared that a new tradition of Battle of Flowers leadership had started.

In 1904 they did an about-face, however, and chose Mrs. John Frazer, a former two-term president, to assume the office. Again she was elected for a second year, but in 1906 the members picked Frank Bushick as their leader. In 1907, Col. George Leroy Brown filled the office, followed in 1908 by Clarence Thomas. He ended the male dynasty, and the Battle of Flowers Association has been exclusively feminine for more than eighty years.

Even before they reverted to electing women to their highest office in 1909, the women had watched their Battle of Flowers grow into a full-fledged *fiesta*. While their parade remained the *pièce de résistance,* now there were several days of varied entertainment. Activities other than the parade had become so numerous and so large that the celebration was difficult to administer.

One who had recognized this problem was Frank Bushick. He had concluded early in his presidency that the ladies needed more support from both sexes. With their blessing, and wide community involvement, he had helped to incorporate a new entity: the Spring Carnival Association. This was accomplished on March 7, 1906. He was named president of the new organization, and the Battle of Flowers became an active member.

Time Brings Changes

In the years between 1891 and the expansion of the Battle of Flowers into the new organization, much had happened to alter the original format. In 1895 the planners seem to have forgotten that their primary purpose was to honor the Alamo dead and the San Jacinto heroes by staging their parade on April 21, the date of the famous fight. Always anxious to attract the largest possible crowds, organizers in 1895 didn't hesitate to switch the Battle of Flowers to June when they learned that a national organization called the Traveler's Protective Association would hold its convention in San Antonio then. They wanted their parade to coincide with this large influx of visitors.

The next year, 1896, the Battle got back on its April schedule and two significant new activities were added. It was the sixtieth anniversary of both the fall of the Alamo and victory at San Jacinto, and the United States finally got around to recognizing these important historical events. Secretary of War Daniel Lamont authorized the firing of a twenty-one-gun salute by the army at Fort Sam Houston. This has been a tradition at the old fort each year since.

Ida Archer may have been one of the most beautiful girls in Texas when she was chosen in 1896 as the first Battle of Flowers Queen. The fact that she was from Austin instead of San Antonio, however, created what the *San Antonio Light* described as "a big row among the fair ones" in the Alamo City. She was the first — and last — "foreign" Queen to occupy the Fiesta throne.

— *Austin History Center*

Queen of a Hostile Realm

The ladies had another idea to enhance the Battle of Flowers. They decided to elect a Queen to rule over the festivities. The idea was welcomed by San Antonio society — until her name was announced. Chosen was Ida Archer, admittedly one of the most beautiful girls in Texas. Her elevation to royal status, however, brought howls of protest from her subjects, especially the local debutantes, and for good reason: Miss Archer was from Austin!

"There is a big row among the fair ones," chortled the *San Antonio Light*. "Out of all of San Antonio's beauties, none were fit to be queen of the charity ball."

It could be argued that Ida Archer was not the *de facto* queen of the Battle of Flowers. That year a charity dance known as the Cotton Ball had been added to the growing number of events and she was chosen to rule with King Cotton (San Antonian Alexander Y. Walton) to enhance that occasion. However, this introduction of royalty to the scene would become another Fiesta tradition over the years.

There were other changes also. By 1896, so many floats had been added to the Battle of Flowers Parade that fresh blossoms no longer were made mandatory. On April 7, the *San Antonio Light* reported that artificial posies as well as fresh flowers would be acceptable as float ornaments.

Today making flowers for the parade has become a cottage industry, and a coterie of women spend at least two months each year producing them for the parade floats. The Battle of Flowers Association also purchased a property where the floats could be built well in advance of the parade date.

Plans for the Battle of Flowers and other Fiesta events are made so carefully and so far in advance that no event except war has ever caused the show to be canceled. That happened in both World Wars, but not in 1898 when the Spanish-American conflict erupted. On February 15, the U.S. battleship *Maine* had been blown up in Havana harbor with 260 Americans killed. Then, on April 21, exactly two hours before the Battle of Flowers parade was to begin, word came that the United States had declared war on Spain.

The city responded with an hour of whistle-blowing and impromptu celebrating. This had an immediate effect on the parade because the military had been a part of it since the beginning. An officer from Fort Sam Houston had been one of the two marshals in the 1891 Battle of Flowers. Since 1892, the Belknap Rifles, a proud militia unit of local volunteers, had marched in the parade each year. Other militia units had also become participants in the event. So, in 1898, the association decided to proceed with the parade despite the declaration of war.

The military always has made important contributions to Fiesta. Here a contingent of U.S. Army Engineers marches in the April 24, 1917, Battle of Flowers, days before leaving for Europe and World War I. The 1898 parade began exactly two hours after the U.S. declared war on Spain. One marching unit, the volunteer Zouaves, halted their march at the Western Union office and telegraphed their enlistments to President William McKinley.
— *Clyde Hester, Institute of Texan Cultures*

Although thousands of bleacher seats are available for Fiesta parades, there also is plenty of standing room along the routes, as shown in this 1941 photo.

— San Antonio Light *Collection,*
Institute of Texan Cultures

From a Parade to the Battlefield

One result was an unplanned patriotic gesture by one of the parade entries that made the front pages of the nation's newspapers. San Antonio at the time had a quasi-military organization known as the Zouaves. As the Battle of Flowers Parade passed in front of the Western Union office, the Zouaves broke ranks, marched inside, and telegraphed their enlistments to President William McKinley.

Their response may have been prompted somewhat by a rumor. The word was that if war came, Theodore Roosevelt, then secretary of the navy, would resign and come to San Antonio for one purpose: He wanted to recruit a special contingent to go to Cuba. Roosevelt missed the Battle of Flowers Parade, but he kept his promise.

Upon resigning his sub-Cabinet post, he hastened to Texas. Using Kampmann's Menger Hotel as a base and its famous bar (modeled after the one in London's House of Lords) as a recruiting station, he enlisted the most famous battle group in the Spanish-American conflict. A San Antonio newspaper helped make the contingent famous by naming them the "Rough Riders."

Despite his fondness for San Antonio, Roosevelt never got back for a Battle of Flowers Parade. However, in 1906, when his Rough Riders held a reunion at the Menger Hotel, he did return. This time he was their commander-in-chief, having assumed the presidency of the United States six years earlier. Many of the women who had helped stage the 1898 parade that produced so many volunteer enlistments for that war attended the dinner that honored him and the heroes of the Battle of San Juan Hill.

War came again eleven years after Roosevelt's memorable visit. Only two weeks before the 1917 Battle of Flowers, President Woodrow Wilson declared war on Germany. The women decided to go forward with their parade anyway, but again the

Thousands of blossoms are necessary to conduct a "battle" of flowers. By 1896, so many floats had been added to the parade and real posies were in such short supply that artificial blooms were permitted for the first time. Today, making ersatz flowers for the parade is a cottage industry in San Antonio.

— *Fiesta San Antonio Commission*

event was given special military significance. Gen. John J. Pershing, who soon would be called from his Fort Sam Houston command to lead the American Expeditionary Forces in Europe, was the honoree at the association's traditional luncheon.

In April 1918 the Battle of Flowers was canceled. World War I occupied the thoughts of everyone and there was no parade. The ladies were not idle, however. They busied themselves knitting for the soldiers, rolling bandages, working in hospitals, volunteering for the Red Cross, and selling War Bonds. They also raised enough money to endow thirty-two beds in an American Army Hospital just outside of Paris.

They did not forget April 21. San Jacinto Day fell on a Sunday, and members of the BOFA took time off from their volunteer war work to join thousands of others in an impromptu pilgrimage to the Alamo. And in 1919, five months after the armi-

stice, the Battle of Flowers became a huge victory parade to the Alamo. There a bronze tablet bearing the names of Bexar County's war dead was unveiled.

With the bombing of Pearl Harbor on December 7, 1941, the Battle of Flowers — indeed, the entire Fiesta — was shelved for four years. Instead of forming their usual committees to produce these events, the BOFA ladies — like "Lucky Strike green" — went to war. They joined the Gray Ladies for hospital duty, trained as nurse's aides, enlisted in the Motor Corps, and volunteered for a variety of jobs.

Even in War, There is Poetry and Oratory

Patriotism and history have been talismen for the Battle of Flowers Association since its beginning, and a world at war didn't shelve all of the organization's projects. In 1923 the group had presented a living picture drama called "Texas Under Six Flags" and had asked one of its members, Mrs. Lawrence Allen Meador, to write a poem as the text. It was so successful that the group offered a prize the next year for the best poem depicting life or historical events in the state's history. There were 265 entries, and the winning author was invited to read her verse at the BOFA annual luncheon.

By 1926, this had evolved into an Oratorical Contest in which the organization offered cash prizes for the speeches on some phase of Texas history. Today the winner of the $1,000 first prize is invited to deliver her speech at the annual luncheon of the Battle of Flowers Association.

At the 1946 luncheon, the delivery of the oration was secondary to the fact that the war had ended and American troops were returning home. It was a triumphant Battle of Flowers, and the entire Fiesta was dedicated to peace. Gen. Jonathan Wainwright, the hero of Bataan and Correigidor who retired in San Antonio, had the place of honor on the reviewing stand for the big parade.

Through wars and peace, the Battle of Flowers Association and its activities continued to expand. Members had decided that they needed a more formalized organization and they applied for a state charter in 1914. The document authorizes an active membership of 400, but the group also has about 120 honorary members. It takes the time, talents, and dedication of each of them to plan and carry out its agenda today.

The Music Goes 'Round and 'Round

Perhaps the most demanding and time-consuming activity next to the Battle of Flowers Parade is the association's Band Festival. It began in the early 1930s as an exhibition performance at Municipal Auditorium Plaza. Held on the morning of April 21, before the big parade, its intent was to showcase the talents of the bands that would be in the march. By 1935, however, it had become an integral part of Fiesta activities and was billed as the "Battle of the Bands." Each group competed for trophies awarded in its division.

Today it is not a competition but a festival to which the participating bands have to be invited. Up to as many as twenty-eight may be asked to perform. Six of the best in or out of San Antonio are chosen as the featured bands and each plays a ten-minute concert. The festival ends with all of the

3,000-plus musicians massing for the finale. The result is reminiscent of the seventy-six trombones that led the big parade in *The Music Man*.

Today the Band Festival is one of the largest of the more than 150 separate events of Fiesta. Not only are there so many musicians on the playing field of Alamo Stadium that there is just enough room for a tuba and a bass drum to turn around, but the 23,000 stadium seats often are also sold out.

However, the Battle of Flowers Parade still takes precedence as the principal crowd-pleaser of them all. The parade likely will remain the premier event and draw Fiesta's largest crowds because it is the occasion when the Queen of the Order of the Alamo and all of her Court can be seen by her thousands of subjects. It is her official parade, and the "ladies in yellow" want to keep it that way.

No Yellow Ribbons?

They want to keep their tradition of wearing yellow too. They insist that their penchant for dressing in this hue does not imply that they are in "uniform." The custom didn't begin until 1970, when Edith C. Sethness, then the BOFA president, was in California to watch the famed Tournament of Roses Parade in Pasadena. She noted that the parade organizers were all dressed in white, making them easily identifiable to the thousands of onlookers. Until then, the Battle of Flowers members had indicated their official status only by wearing white sashes with their dresses.

When President Sethness returned home, she suggested that the BOFA adopt yellow as their color. Not all agreed. Some preferred pink. Others objected because they felt that yellow is unflattering to certain skin tones. Not a few said that it simply looked "sickly." The majority, however, agreed with their leader and yellow, in any of its varied hues, was accepted in 1971.

Members may wear yellow skirts and blouses, dresses with short or no sleeves, and straight or full skirts in any shade they choose. In the 100-plus temperatures that often warm the Battle of Flowers, cool Mexican dresses have become a favorite. But in the matter of hats, the members have no choice. Each must sport a wide-brimmed, garden-party-type hat. Between public appearances, the hats are stored at BOFA headquarters in the charge of one of the members.

Each April 21, the hats come out of storage. The bright yellow straws are required apparel at all times on the day of the Battle of Flowers Parade.

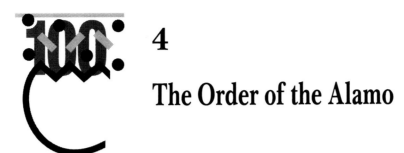

4

The Order of the Alamo

"There wouldn't be half as much fun in the world if it weren't for children and men, and there ain't a mite of difference between them under their skins."

— Ellen Glasgow, American novelist

Although the Battle of Flowers Parade, A Night in Old San Antonio, and much of the pomp and circumstance of Fiesta San Antonio were created by, and are still the province of, the ladies, men have a major role in the celebration too.

It should be remembered that the idea for this annual festivity originated with a man visiting from Chicago, and that it was the president of the city's exclusive all-male club who recruited the funds and the masculine muscle needed to make the first Battle of Flowers possible.

Fiesta's debt extends to more than one such organization. Clubs — especially those which admit only men — have been a binding tie for the local socially elite since 1854, when twenty prominent Germans formed the Casino Association. Termed San Antonio's "first respectable social club" by its founders, its goal was to perpetuate German culture. It was, as local historian Charles Ramsdell wrote, "the greatest source for culture the city ever had." It might still be today if Prohibition had not forced it to close in 1923 and sell the building in which it had staged operas, musicals, lectures, and masked balls. Many of these were rather like miniatures of some Fiesta activities.

In the club-oriented city that is San Antonio, however, there is always another prestigious group ready to step into any vacuum that may occur. And fourteen years before the demise of the Casino Association, the Order of the Alamo had been organized. Today many San Antonians consider this group as representative of local society at its best. It has no club house, meets only once a year, and has membership restrictions as demanding as those of the fraternities that most of the Order of the Alamo members pledged at the University of Texas,

Princeton, Washington and Lee, or some other prestigious school.

The Order of the Alamo certainly is not the only exclusive men's organization in San Antonio. Later its founder, John Carrington, would form the Cavaliers, which draws its much larger membership from the same social strata. Between the two organizations, they control who shall occupy the thrones of the major Fiesta royalty. The Queen and her Court are the province of the Order of the Alamo, and the Cavaliers select the King. For reasons never made clear, these rulers are invested in separate coronations, although both reign over the same loyal subjects — the thousands who annually participate in some phase of Fiesta San Antonio.

"We do nothing . . . and do it well"

Another exclusive group, the Conopus Club, is an interesting hybrid that draws most of its 210 members from the Order of the Alamo and the Cavaliers. Unlike the first two, however, Conopus as an organization has no active role in Fiesta. In fact, its motto is: "We do nothing and do it well." It even discourages members' attendance at its weekly luncheons at the San Antonio Country Club, although they are billed for the meal when they are absent. (Missing the lunch builds up the club's treasury, which is spent later on parties.) Nevertheless, most members of Conopus, as scions of San Antonio's society, are involved in one or more of Fiesta's events through their affinity with either the Order of the Alamo, the Cavaliers, or both.

Long before any of these groups came into being, San Antonio men had formed innumerable societies and associations serving a variety of inter-

Eda Kampmann, first Queen selected by the Order of the Alamo in 1909. A descendant of an old and prominent San Antonio family, her mother, Mrs. H. D. Kampmann, was the first president of the Battle of Flowers Association, which started Fiesta in 1891.

— Photo courtesy of Ike D. Kampmann

ests. Like the Casino Association, not all have weathered the vicissitudes of time. One that has endured is the San Antonio Club, in whose sacred male precincts the ladies laid the first plans for their Battle of Flowers. Others have not been so fortunate. The 1852 Club finally gave up the ghost because there were no new members to take in. Only those born in 1852 could join!

Whether they belonged to a restricted social clique or not, individual men have always had an important, if often behind-the-scenes, role in Fiesta. However, the Order of the Alamo was the first all-male sodality with a single purpose: to plan and execute a specific aspect of Fiesta. Members select and direct the coronation and entertainment of the Queen and her court.

The Man Who Changed San Antonio Society

This tightly knit, exclusive society of gentlemen-in-waiting to Her Royal Majesty might never have existed except for the arrival in San Antonio of John Baron Carrington about the turn of the century. Carrington was the founder, architect, inspirer, and first president of what he called the Order of the Alamo.

Carrington was the type of new citizen that any community is proud to welcome, and his acceptance by the local aristocracy was immediate and warm. His credentials were impeccable: like so many of the leading citizens in his newly adopted home city, he was descended from Old South stock. In his native Halifax County, the Carringtons were FFV — a First Family of Virginia. That alone insured that the social elite of San Antonio would open their hearts and doors to him.

He, in turn, responded enthusiastically, involving himself in a variety of business and community activities. Something of an entrepreneur, he founded one of the first neon sign companies in Texas, then engaged for a while in investment counseling and later edited a local publication.

Recognized by his fellow citizens as a born leader, the peripatetic Carrington was chosen as executive secretary of the Chamber of Commerce in 1909 — one of two stints totaling eleven years in which he served the business community as its principal spokesman. By the time he assumed the Chamber office, the Battle of Flowers had grown into a small but full-fledged Fiesta. Joining with other male volunteers, he had been a part of this growth since his arrival in town. Now, as the paid executive of the Chamber, he believed that one of

John Baron Carrington, founder of both the Order of the Alamo and the Cavaliers. He not only revolutionized Fiesta but changed San Antonio society at the same time.

— Photo courtesy of Pauline Carrington James

his primary efforts should be to help develop Fiesta into an even larger and more important celebration.

To accomplish this, he set out to involve more men directly in the annual event.

There was an established precedent for his idea. As related earlier, women organizing the Battle of Flowers decided in 1901 to let men worry about financing the parade while they devoted their time to social amenities. To divide these responsibilities, they chose a male as their president. This eventually led to the organization in 1906 of a new group called the Spring Carnival Association, which took over the full responsibility for all aspects of Fiesta.

The Ups and Downs of Royalty

Carrington supported the new association and applauded the fact that it welcomed both sexes as members. However, he believed that something more was needed. As executive secretary of the Chamber, he was acutely aware of the social significance of Fiesta and believed that not enough importance had been attached to selecting a Queen.

Dignitaries riding in early Battle of Flowers parades rode in automobiles decked out in a variety of posies.
— *Ann Russell Collection, Institute of Texan Cultures*

Joe H. Frost, shown at the controls of a biplane in 1916, was one of the prominent leaders John Carrington enlisted in forming the Order of the Alamo. His flying instructor was Marjorie Stinson who, at fourteen, became America's youngest licensed pilot. In 1912, Frost married Eda Kampmann, the first Queen to be selected by the Order.

— *Institute of Texan Cultures*

Until Carrington's arrival, Fiesta royalty had been an off-again, on-again affair. The tradition had started fourteen years earlier, in 1896, when the beautiful Ida Archer of Austin had been chosen, to the consternation of San Antonio debutantes. The following year, the sponsors mended their ways and selected a local beauty, May Cresson, to reign. They even gave her a consort: King Clinton Kearney.

By 1898, however, males eligible for elevation to temporary royal status either had enlisted in the army in anticipation of war with Spain or were planning to do so. No King of Fiesta was chosen, but Miss Helen McLeary was selected as Queen. By the 1899 Fiesta, Teddy Roosevelt and his San Antonio-recruited Rough Riders had stormed victoriously up Cuba's San Juan Hill, the war was over, and George Gosling shared the throne with Queen Emma Reed.

Still the choosing of Fiesta royalty was not a "must" item on the agenda of the Battle of Flowers. In 1902 and 1903, during the presidencies of two of the six males who headed the BOFA, there were neither Queens nor Kings. Then when Mrs. Frazer took over in 1904 for a double term, there was a Queen for each of the two years — but it was the same young lady. In fact, she would wear the crown a third year (see the following chapter on the Queens).

John Carrington insisted that Fiesta royalty resemble the real thing as closely as possible. Here Ray Baldus displays replicas of the gems worn by England's Queen Victoria. These were worn by the Empress of Golconda in the 1926 Coronation.

— San Antonio Light *Collection,
Institute of Texan Cultures*

Setting the Path to Fiesta's Throne

This informal way of selecting royalty weighed on an organized mind like Carrington's. And he believed that the selection of a Queen was as important to the future of Fiesta as the Battle of Flowers Parade and too important to leave to chance or a whim. Long before he assumed his Chamber of Commerce position, he had thought of forming an organization whose only responsibility would be the choosing, coronation, and care of a young lady to rule over the event. He had discussed this with other community leaders and found immediate support from at least two of the city's most prominent citizens, J. H. Frost and Franz Groos. They represented the moneyed, socially elite group which Carrington felt should have the responsibility for choosing Fiesta's royal family.

That both the Battle of Flowers and the Spring Carnival Association were in place and that Queens had been chosen by the previous group for several years did not deter Carrington. He believed that a third organization was needed, and he set about its establishment.

Selecting the first group of eminent young men to embrace the Order of the Alamo was not difficult. Although there was no San Antonio Social Register at the time, and today's ultra exclusive Argyle Club was still a hotel on the outskirts of downtown, putting together a list of the elite was easy. Everybody who was anybody knew who really belonged to the limited social circle. Also, the San Antonio Country Club, still the bastion of the local elite, had opened two years earlier on 135 acres at Hildebrand and New Braunfels.

The Gentlemen-in-Waiting Are Organized

It was from the country club roster and word-of-mouth recommendations from old families that Carrington chose the first sixty-three members of the group he called the Order of the Alamo. He intended that the membership would never exceed 100.

The 1909 Fiesta was almost upon them by the time the Order of the Alamo got organized, and President Carrington gave the gentlemen their assignments. They had to select the Queen, the Dukes and Duchesses from around the state, the other Lords and Ladies-in-waiting and the complete Court, and plan all entertainment and other activities. They elected the Court of Springtime as the theme and Eda Kampmann, daughter of the first chairman of the Battle of Flowers, as their Queen. Beethoven Hall, then as now a cultural oasis, was chosen for the Coronation. The following night, there was a ball in her honor.

Although Miss Kampmann was from one of the richest families in San Antonio, wealth, or the lack of it, has never been given undue importance by the Order of the Alamo in selecting the Queen and her Court. Members of the Order don't discuss outside their secret meetings how they go about the process. They do insist, however, that money isn't the criterion in choosing the young ladies on which they confer San Antonio's highest social honor. Heritage — interpreted as "family" — is!

Since the Order of the Alamo assumed responsibility for the Coronation and the selection of its royalty, the process has undergone minor changes. In the beginning, each member voted in the Queen's election. In 1912 it was decided that this important decision should be made only by the Board of Directors. That was changed again a decade later when the Order's constitution was amended to provide for three candidates for the throne.

Still later another change was made in the method of selection. Now there is no list of candidates. Each member may vote for any three young ladies, listing them in the order of his preference. The ballots have to be delivered in person at a secret meeting. The new Queen is the one receiving the most votes, and the runner-up is the Princess.

The Queen is Chosen at the Alamo

The Queen's election is held at the Alamo in the month of December. In 1922 the Order met for the first time in the shrine and decided that henceforth the annual session to choose royalty would be held in the famed Chapel. However, even with the ghosts of the Alamo heroes hovering about, the selection is never an easy task.

For example, the Minutes of the 1915 meeting reported that "the Town Court Committee, after debating four hours and twenty minutes, elected the following Duchesses." Some sessions have taken even longer.

The 100th anniversary Fiesta in 1991 will mark the eighty-second year that the Order of the Alamo has been responsible for the Coronation. Except for 1918, 1919, 1943, 1944, and 1945 (the years of World Wars I and II) this event has been the central focus of the celebration. During the First World War, more than forty members of the Order of the Alamo were in uniform. The organization put its entire treasury into Liberty Bonds, except for a sum used to endow a bed at the American Hospital in Neuilly-Sur-Seine outside of Paris.

On December 8, 1941 — the day after Pearl Harbor — the Order met at the Alamo. The theme for the 1942 Coronation had been selected. It was to be the "Court of Holidays." A Queen, Carrie Louise Kuntz, had been chosen. Only the Duchesses and other members of the Court remained to be named. However, with war declared and 126 members of the Order either in uniform or about to be, Albert Steves III moved that "no formal Coronation be held in the Spring." It was passed unanimously.

War Changes Everything

Weekly meetings of the Board of Directors continued. No Princess was appointed nor were other members of the Court. Like the Order of the Alamo, many members of the Cavaliers were either already in one of the armed services or else preparing to go. They did not name a King. The only function was a Queen's Ball at which Miss Kuntz was crowned in a simple ceremony.

Since World War II, the Queen and King Coronations no longer are the unsophisticated affairs that they once were. The ceremonies themselves are so elaborate that they could be stage settings for a motion picture. Two of the most coveted social invitations of the year are to events attendant to the Coronation: the Queen's Garden Party and the Queen's Ball. The ball, always held at the Menger Hotel, requires the entire first floor. Both events are sponsored by the Order of the Alamo.

5

The Queens

"The Queen — Now can you guess who that could be?"

— Rose Fyleman in *The Fairies*

San Antonio is but one of many American cities that boast a long tradition of elevating one of their own to temporary royal status.

St. Louis has its Queen of the Veiled Prophet Ball, New Orleans its Kings of Mardi Gras, Pasadena its Queen of the Tournament of Roses, and so on. In Texas alone, in 1990, almost 1,000 Queens, Kings and uncounted Princesses and Duchesses were chosen to occupy, if only for a day or two, the royal realm in their home towns.

The Lone Star State claims to lead the nation in the production of cattle, cotton, and festivals. The Fire Ant Festival in Marshall, the Great Mosquito Festival in Clute, and the more than 500 similar events held each year around the state may not have the pomp and circumstance of Fiesta San Antonio, but each is unique in its own way. For example, at the Citrus Fiesta in Mission, its Empress, King, and Princesses wear costumes decorated with harvest products like congealed orange juice, onion skins, and lemon peels — hardly the *haute couture* employed in designing the gowns of the Queen chosen by the Order of the Alamo.

Most of the state's festivals are satisfied to have only one Queen per event, but not San Antonio. In today's Fiesta there are two Kings — one the traditional Antonio and the other El Rey Feo (the Ugly King). Some of the military installations choose a Queen, but most now select both a male and female as "representatives" to Fiesta. There is a Miss Fiesta, plus a Queen of Soul. It used to be that only the Fiesta Commission staff knew in advance how much royalty there would be. This is no longer true. The number of Queens and Kings who can participate in Fiesta was frozen in the 1980s.

However, this profusion of crowned heads can still be confusing, and not only to the coalition of old San Antonio families of wealth and aristocracy from which the principal Queen and King have always come. The more than 500,000 visitors who converge on the Alamo City during Fiesta express wonder when as many as eight Queens appear in a single parade.

It was not always so. For many years, only one Queen was selected (for the Battle of Flowers). In most, but not all, years there also was a King. In the late 1940s the custom of selecting a "Miss Fiesta" began. However, there is no one set of royalty that outranks another. In the 1970s, the Fiesta San Antonio Commission issued a fiat stating that no one set of royalty can "rule over" the celebration. Thus began the proliferation of beautiful young ladies wearing the crowns of a variety of realms.

The One True Queen?

Nevertheless, members of the Order of the Alamo (which select the Queen), or of the Cavaliers (who choose the King), will argue that the "true" royal dynasty in San Antonio is the one their organizations have controlled for decades. Most San Antonians agree. It is the formal Coronation of the Queen in a glittering public ceremony and the elevation of the King to his throne in solemn Alamo rites that win the attention of the media and the public.

It is also on these two sovereigns, and their courts, that the spotlight is focused in two major Fiesta events. The Battle of Flowers Parade is that of the traditional Queen and her Court. The River Parade was King Antonio's showcase until he elected to share it in 1989 with El Rey Feo, the Ugly King.

Above: In the 1920s, even the high schools elected their own Fiesta royalty and staged parades. Here the Queens and their courts from all of the city's schools pose with two Cavalier escorts.

— *Lewiston photo from the San Antonio Museum Association Collection*

Below: The Queen selected by the Order of the Alamo is but one of many royal ladies who rule over Fiesta. The nine Queens above represented various Army and Air Force installations in the city during one celebration.

— *U.S. Army photograph*

There is considerable precedent for the acceptance of the Alamo's Queen and the Cavalier's King as the "true" royalty. Since 1909, not only the Queen but her entire Court — the Princesses, Duchesses, Dukes, Prime Minister, the Lord High Chamberlain, and even the Pages — have been chosen by the Order of the Alamo. To be chosen to reign as Queen of Fiesta has always meant the highest honor that San Antonio society can bestow on one of its debutantes.

Ostensibly there are no rules that govern admission to the Court of the Alamo's Queen (at least, they're not made public). It is assumed, however, that membership in the inner circle of old aristocracy is a requirement. Certainly, twelve months as a Princess or Duchess of Fiesta is a rite of passage that almost guarantees the lucky young lady a special place in San Antonio society for all time to come.

On the other hand, there is no direct procession to the Fiesta throne. Having once been a Queen is no guarantee that, in time, a daughter may succeed the mother. However, when the list of new royalty is announced each year, it always includes the names of daughters, granddaughters, and even nieces of former Queens, Princesses, and Duchesses.

The Road to Royalty

Heritage, not money, has been the principal criterion considered by the Order of the Alamo when they meet in secret at the historic shrine each year to select the Queen and her Court. San Antonio has never been a moneyed town in the sense that New York, Dallas, Houston, and many other cities are. There is a good deal of wealth, to be sure, but it doesn't buy its way into the San Antonio Social Register. (In fact, the city never had such a publication until the 1980s.) More than one father of a Queen, Princess, or Duchess has been hard-pressed to come up with the $5,000 to $50,000 and more which these ten days of royalty can cost participants.

So how does one of the city's most beautiful win the blessing of the Order of the Alamo and become one of its Court?

Although being a descendant of one of the "first families" (those who came after statehood in 1845 and before 1900) is a help, it is not an absolute requirement. If there have been other Queens, Princesses, or Duchesses from the family since 1896 (the first year the Battle of Flowers had royalty),

Battle of Flowers Queens chosen in 1896 through 1899 wore evening gowns and were crowned in a simple ceremony at the Alamo. However, in 1900, when Lola Kokernot (above) was chosen Queen, she was the first to have a court with a Princess, Duchesses, and other attendants. The Coronation began moving toward the extravaganza that it is today.

— San Antonio Museum Association Collection

that is a plus. Whether the family name is on the roster of the "right" clubs (the Argyle, San Antonio Country Club and, in recent years, the Club Giraud) is checked. Then there is the family's support of cultural activities like the symphony, the mother's membership (or lack of it) in the Junior League — all of these, and more, are important.

Even having been a Page in a past Court counts. A German Club debut isn't required, but it adds points in the selection process. Being chosen as Princess, or a Duchess at least, means that the gate to the Queen's throne is not closed.

From then on, it's up to the members of the Order of the Alamo. Having a father who is a member doesn't hurt. Neither does it guarantee selection.

The First Coronation

Making the right choice of their first Queen in 1909 was of primary importance to the Order of the Alamo. In choosing Eda Kampmann for the honor,

Being Queen of Fiesta is an experience traditionally reserved for a San Antonio debutante. After the protests that greeted the selection of Ida Archer from Austin as the first Queen, it was assumed that future royalty would always be from San Antonio. But Clara Driscoll, who reigned for three successive years as Queen, hailed from Corpus Christi, though she called San Antonio home.

— Institute of Texan Cultures

the Order of the Alamo set the criteria for future occupants of the throne. She was both beautiful and a member of one of the "first families" of San Antonio — two qualities by which Queens are still measured.

For more than forty years before the first Battle of Flowers, the Kampmanns had been a powerful family in San Antonio. Eda's grandfather, John Herman Kampmann, is still remembered as one of the city's greatest builders. A self-taught architect, he migrated from his native Westphalia, Prussia, to Texas in 1846, entering at the port of Indianola. He then traveled for two weeks by ox cart to join the new German settlement that had been established at New Braunfels by Prince Carl of Solms-Braunfels.

Soon he was busy designing and erecting structures like the General Land Office in Austin and the Bastrop County Courthouse. He became the builder of San Antonio's Menger Hotel, a structure that he would later buy and operate; founded and built the Lone Star Brewery; organized and became president of the San Antonio Gas Company; and developed myriad business interests around the state. His son, Herman, married Elizabeth Simpson, daughter of a prominent judge. Mrs. Kampmann would become the first president of the Battle of Flowers, and her daughter, Eda, the first Queen of the Order of the Alamo.

Growth of a Dynasty

The selection of the Kampmanns' daughter as Queen, and the choice of the members of her Court, began the strong tradition of family that has been a part of Fiesta royalty. On a list of the hundreds who have been a part of the Queen's court in the last century, the names of old San Antonio families occur with clocklike frequency. Armstrong, Carr, Clegg, Denman, Groos, Guenther, Heard, Herff, Kampmann, Kleberg, McAllister, Nixon, Seeligson, Simpson, Steves, Terrell, and many others are there.

This has prompted some to observe that San Antonio's old families have always had a kind of royal dynasty going. The Order of the Alamo emphasizes that the Coronation is a tradition handed down from generation to generation, and the Queen invariably is from one of the families who represent both the social elite and old money.

That the Coronation is intended to be something of a family affair is emphasized in one of the books issued by the Order of the Alamo to com-

Costumes for the Queen, the Princess, and her Duchesses are the responsibility of the Mistress of Robes, who must approve all designs. In the Court of India in 1933, Marjory Ripley, representing the U.S. Army, is costumed as the Rani of Bhutan.

— Cones photo from the San Antonio Museum Association Collection

Above: Lola Kokernot, the first Queen to have a court, is crowned in a 1900 ceremony. She shared the throne with King Thomas Conroy. Modern coronations do not include the King. Antonio ascends to his rule in solemn, closed ceremonies at the Alamo attended only by his fellow Cavaliers.

— San Antonio Light *Collection, Institute of Texan Cultures*

Below: The Lord Chamberlain of the Order of the Alamo places the crown on Queen Margaret Charlisa Walker in April 1941. Queen Margaret Charlisa presided over the Court of Legends. Her throne is flanked by giant candlesticks and books of legends, typical of the elaborate stagecraft used in Fiesta coronations.

— *San Antonio Museum Association*

memorate the royal realms for which it has been responsible. In an introduction, the anonymous author writes: "Many a Duchess, Princess or Queen recalls an earlier day in another Court when she toddled along as a page or entertainer. As she watched in amazement the dazzling spectacle before her, she dreamed, never realizing that it could come true, of a day in which she might be proclaimed and honored in such a way."

Children who were Pages or other attendants do grow up to be Kings, Queens, Princesses, Dukes, or Lords, often as members of several different courts. In 1909, Julia Armstrong was a Princess and maid of honor to Queen Eda Kampmann. In 1910 and 1911, she held a lesser role at the Court as a Duchess. But in 1912, after three years in the assembly of nobles, she assumed the throne as Queen of the Court of Lilies.

Something Old, Something New?

Whether the reason was economic or otherwise, Miss Armstrong apparently felt no reason to compete with other members of the Court in trying to outdo each other in fashions. For three consecutive years, she wore the same gown at the Coronation! It was not until her selection as Queen that she appeared at the ceremony in something new.

Actually, the clothing worn by Queens in early Coronations apparently was of no great concern. Even after the Order of the Alamo assumed the responsibility for selecting Queens, a participant simply chose a fashionable dress that could be a permanent addition to her wardrobe.

This lack of emphasis on fashion changed quickly. It was John Baron Carrington, founder of the Order and its first president, who was responsible for making the Coronation the elaborate, expensive affair that it remains today. As a migrant from Virginia aristocracy, Carrington had a predilection for an era long gone — the Age of Chivalry. He decreed that the crowning of the Queen of Fiesta should be a ceremony patterned after similar rites for a European head of state.

Although that first Coronation staged at Beethoven Hall lacked much of the pretense and ostentation that are hallmarks of the event today, it was a beginning. If the investiture ceremonies of "Miss Eda" (as even her suitors addressed her) were relatively simple compared with the present Coronation extravaganza, they set a precedent that still is evolving.

The Coronation Today

While the presentation has become increasingly lavish over the years, much of it has remained unchanged. The Order of the Alamo has never deviated from Carrington's idea of using a theme for the show that has more than a tinge of make-believe. Apparently, Carrington loved flowers as much as he did the tradition of chivalry, and he decided that Queen Eda should rule over the Court of Flowers. The next year, it was Roses, then the Carnival of Flowers followed by the Lilies of Spring. In 1914 it was the Court of the Year, and in intervening years there have been Courts of the Universe, the Birds, the Old South, Holidays, and more.

Whatever the theme, the Queen, the Princess, and each Duchess is given a title that relates to it. The challenge then is to design dresses that can be adorned in ways to emphasize the theme. This can be a difficult task. For example, in the 1952 Court of Make Believe, there were Duchesses of the Snow Queen, the White Cat, Cinderella, and Nixie of the Mill Pond, among others.

The public program also is carefully scripted to carry out the theme. Although the emphasis is on the royalty, there is first-rate entertainment for the "commoners" in the audience. This often is presented as the warm-up before the Lord Chamberlain, the individual selected by the chairman of the Coronation Committee to serve as master of ceremonies, takes over.

King Antonio, already crowned by the Cavaliers in an Alamo ceremony, attends along with El Rey Feo, who was crowned the previous August. Following their introductions, they and their parties are shown to their seats. With the rest of the audience, they watch the Coronation begin with the entrance of the visiting Duchesses who have been invited from other cities. They are followed by the local Duchesses in elegant gowns ornamented with jewels in intricate designs depicting the Court theme each represents. They make a formal court bow, then are escorted to their seats by a Duke.

A Bit of Old England

Trumpets announce the Queen's entrance. Preceded by her guard and pages, she walks to the highest platform on the stage and kneels before the president of the Order of the Alamo. Until 1925, she always entered wearing her crown. But since British royalty always is crowned in London's Westminster Abbey by the Archbishop of Canterbury, Carrington decided to follow English tradition as closely as possible. He had the script rewritten, making the president of the Order assume temporarily the dual role of Archbishop.

Today, however, the president uses only the prerogative of his elected office and proclaims the Queen, then reads to her a long and very formal oath. When she responds with the required "I do," he places the crown on her head and hands her the scepter that is the symbol of her authority. For the next twelve months, she will rule whatever Court the Order has ordained as the theme until next Fiesta.

The Coronation sets off days of hectic activity. The Queen will spend her days making some of the tours to schools, nursing homes, hospitals, and other places with King Antonio. There will be constant luncheons, dinners, and TV appearances. Then come the Queen's Garden Party, the Queen's Ball (the Menger Hotel has been a favorite location), the Battle of Flowers Parade, and more.

Who Pays for It and How Much?

What does it cost to stage the Coronation? That is one of the closely guarded secrets of the Order of the Alamo, but certainly it adds up to thousands of dollars. Loyal subjects who attend pay for their seats, and the Fiesta Commission helps out with a grant.

When it comes to costuming the Queen, however, it's the family who pays. And the price for the Coronation regalia alone can cost $25,000 and up.

It wasn't always so. As pointed out earlier, when Ida Archer was the first Queen of the Battle of Flowers in 1891, she wore a fashionable gown that might have come from her own wardrobe. During the early years of Fiesta royalty, Queens followed Miss Archer's precedent. If short dresses were in vogue, then the royal hemline was also short. As befitting one new to the throne, however, the Coronation gown usually was embellished with a train and otherwise made more ostentatious. At least half a century passed before the Queen's Coronation robes became the expensive, showy creations that they are today.

The professional producers of the Coronation set rationalize the sumptuous, colorful, rhinestone-studded gowns by saying that they have to be designed for stage presentation. The idea is to make them highly visible to the 3,500 who pay hit show prices for their seats and expect an extravaganza for their money. To make sure that all of the finery worn by the entire Court shall never disappoint, the Order of the Alamo annually selects the individual that is a Fiesta necessity: the Mistress of the Robes.

Not Available in Ready-to-Wear

A new Mistress is appointed by the Coronation chairman as long as two years before the Coronation over which she will preside as arbiter of dress. To be selected Mistress of Robes is a coveted honor, although it is probably the hardest, most tedious of all Fiesta assignments. Experience has shown that the Mistress needs at least a full year to carry out her duties (more than one past Mistress says she wished for even more time). She and the chairman are personally responsible for overseeing the design of each gown and to make sure that it is executed exactly. Many of the intricate garments can take up to six months to produce.

The process begins when the Order of the Alamo selects those who will be members of the Court. Those chosen meet with the Mistress of the Robes to decide on the design of their dresses and determine how they can be integrated into the theme of the next Coronation. Once these decisions are made and there is the certainty that the family won't be forced into involuntary bankruptcy by the expenditure, a dressmaker is chosen. Only those approved in advance by the Order can take the assignment.

Over the next weeks and months, the responsibility of the Mistress is arduous. She has to keep a watchful eye on each step as the seamstress creates the robe, making suggestions and revisions when necessary. Each gown requires four to six fittings with the Mistress in attendance. No Duchess, or even the Queen and her Princess, may appear at the Coronation until the Mistress of the Robes has given her final approval to the royal raiment.

Three Times a Queen

Fortunately, for both the young lady's well-being and her family's pocketbook, being crowned Queen of Fiesta is a once-in-a-lifetime experience. But one repeater occupied the throne for three consecutive years. She was also the only Queen besides Ida Archer who didn't call San Antonio home.

She was Clara Driscoll of Corpus Christi, daughter of a rich ranching family with close ties to San Antonio. Although educated largely in New

York and France, Clara regarded San Antonio as a kind of second home and was well known in local society. The Driscolls were considered a part of the Alamo City's "inner circle," which may explain why there was no cry raised when she was chosen for royal status in 1904 over local debutantes who hoped for honor.

That Miss Driscoll was selected Queen again in 1905 and still again in 1906 might have raised some eyebrows except for one development: When she ascended the throne, she began a fight that was to focus national attention on her and her adopted city of San Antonio and give her a unique niche in history as "the savior of the Alamo."

Liquor Store or Shrine?

Probably because of her frequent stays at the Kampmanns' Menger Hotel on the plaza opposite the Alamo, Clara Driscoll had developed an interest in the old mission and its future. Like every Texan, she knew how the first Battle of the Alamo had lasted only thirteen days. But unlike most other Texans of the time, she couldn't understand why so little had been done to preserve the shrine for posterity.

Since the famed siege that had seen 189 of its defenders slaughtered by General Santa Anna's Mexican army, the Alamo had been largely neglected. In 1841 the Republic of Texas gave the famous building and the other San Antonio missions back to the Roman Catholic Church. The church, in turn, leased the property to the U.S. government, and the Alamo became a quartermaster depot for the army.

It remained so until the Civil War, when the Confederates took it over. When peace came, it reverted to the U.S. Then, in 1877, the Catholic Church sold it to a San Antonio businessman and it became a wholesale grocery and liquor warehouse. In 1903, when it was rumored that it would be sold again, then razed so that a hotel could be built on the property, the new Queen of Fiesta went into action.

She put up $75,000 of her own money and took an option on the Alamo, holding it long enough to preserve it from destruction. This precipitated "the second Battle of the Alamo" — a fight that divided San Antonians into one camp that hoped to save the shrine and another that wanted to see a commercial building on the site.

It also caused a split in the Daughters of the Republic of Texas who, while almost unanimous in

The road to the Queen's throne starts early, usually as an attendant at court. The seemingly uninterested page in this 1956 picture may be a future King Antonio in the making.

— San Antonio Express/News *Collection, Institute of Texan Cultures*

their desire to save the Alamo, violently disagreed on who should own and control it. One faction followed Adina de Zavala, who first sounded the alarm over the commercialization of the shrine. Years of hassles and court fights were to follow before the issue was settled and the Alamo was saved. But it was Miss Driscoll who provided the money that finally saved the Alamo.

In her book, *The Battle of Flowers Association,* Mary Etta McGimsey credits Miss Driscoll's unprecedented selection for a third year as Queen to her preservation endeavors: "This signal honor was bestowed upon Miss Driscoll because of her great patriotic efforts to recover the Alamo property from private ownership to State custody. During these three years, the coronation ceremonies took place in front of the Alamo."

Miss Driscoll's occupancy of the Fiesta throne, made different by her own nonresidency within her royal realm, also involved a King who some regarded as an "outsider." He was Judge Clarence

Martin of Fredericksburg. He shared the throne in 1904. In the other two years of her reign, however, her Kings were from old San Antonio families: J. D. Woodward in 1905 and Arthur Guenther in 1906.

No More "Foreign" Royalty

No future Queen shall be able to duplicate Miss Driscoll's feat and serve more than once on the throne. And the Order of the Alamo has made sure that she shall always be a hometown girl. From the time of Clara Driscoll's selection, the matter of the eligibility of Fiesta royalty was under discussion. Finally, in 1923, the Order amended its by-laws to require the Princess to have been a Bexar County resident for at least three years. Duchesses are required to have only one year of local residence. No citizenship requirement was set for the Queen, but most regard that as a moot question since she is invariably chosen from the Duchessess of a previous Court.

Although it's a certainty that the choice will be made from less than a dozen debutantes, there is still a spring guessing game as to who the new Queen will be. Until the Coronation, her identity is always one of the city's best-kept secrets.

There are those who question why the ostentatious Coronation of a beautiful debutante should be a part of Fiesta. They argue that it isn't worth the time, effort, and expense. Obviously the Order of the Alamo and San Antonio society think that it is. After all, April is a magic time in San Antonio, made so by the weather, the wealth of flowers, and the ten days of parties and parades known as Fiesta. And since the City of the Alamo does become a kind of make-believe kingdom for those few days each spring, why not have a temporary royal family to rule over it?

By enthroning a Queen and a King for even a brief reign each year, John Carrington hoped to carry their subjects back in time to a never-never land and to allow a brief escape from everyday real-

In 1922, Queen Eugenia Taylor of the Court of Aladdin pauses to smile at the photographer before going for a drive in her official touring car. A gallant aide holds the royal train over his shoulder and his straw bowler in the other hand.

— San Antonio Museum Association

ity. Since the beginning of recorded time, people have sought such a nirvana. To the American hobo of the 1930s, it was expressed in the ballad, "The Big Rock Candy Mountain," a place where "there's birds and bees and cigaret trees and lemonade springs" and life was perfect. To San Antonio, with its long Hispanic heritage, Fiesta may not be perfect, but *"es ambiente."*

Who could ask for anything more?

6

The Texas Cavaliers

"Cavalier — a courtly or dashing gentleman; a gallant; a lady's escort."
— The Reader's Digest Great Encyclopedic Dictionary

To John Baron Carrington, the upper-class Virginian who immigrated to Texas and proceeded to change San Antonio's society, Fiesta, for all of its success, lacked an important ingredient: gentility.

The brainchild of the city's old patrician society, the original Battle of Flowers had grown each year in number of participants and those who watched the parade. To Carrington, however, the event had become like a raucous carnival rather than what he envisioned a celebration sponsored by the gentry should be. While he strongly supported increasing its diversions and the involvement of every sector of the population, he felt that an important part of the merriment should focus on the aristocracy that had been its originators.

He had begun the process in 1909 when, as secretary of the Chamber of Commerce, he had founded the prestigious Order of the Alamo with one goal: to select and crown a Queen each year. He had limited membership in the Order to carefully selected gentlemen from old, well established San Antonio families. They, in turn, had chosen as their Queens the finest representatives of local society. In the years that the Order had assumed this responsibility, it had, in Carrington's view, brought at least a modicum of nobility to Fiesta.

For all their good works, however, members of the Order of the Alamo mildly disappointed their founder and first president. Although most had grown up in the heart of the Texas ranch country where the horse was almost a necessity of life, few of his Alamo recruits were expert riders. Like most Texans, they hunted deer and quail, many on their own ranches, and probably considered themselves "gentlemen sportsmen." But that term had a different meaning to Carrington.

In the Old Virginia where he grew up, the primary upper-class sporting event required donning a red coat, black boots, and an English cap and riding a thoroughbred horse behind a pack of registered dogs which chased a fox. Carrington recognized that while Virginia's meadows and rolling hills were the perfect setting for such hunts, the brush country south and west of San Antonio was not. Although a haven for deer, javelina and other game, including coyotes and an occasional wildcat, it was not the province of the red fox.

If Carrington could not add fox hunting as a class event for Fiesta, he decided he could do something even more exciting. He had been fascinated from boyhood with medieval history and loved to read of the derring-do of knights in armor. Why not organize a contingent of blue-blooded Texans who could prove their mettle in jousting for the entertainment of the Queen of Fiesta?

The Cavaliers Take the Field

An organization of Cavaliers was his answer. Even the name itself would appeal, he was confident, to the many-sided ethnic population of the city. The French had their *chevaliers* and the Spanish their *caballeros*. Like the English cavalier, the words in each language imply "knighthood." And the literal translation of the Spanish *caballero* is "man on horseback." Since Carrington most of all wanted "to preserve the Texas tradition of horsemanship in this age of automobiles," as he phrased it, he hoped to use the Cavaliers to accomplish this purpose.

So the Cavaliers were chartered on April 12, 1926, seventeen years after Carrington had organized the Order of the Alamo. He made his purposes clear to the nineteen men he selected as the first members. They would have three primary objectives: First, to sponsor a pilgrimage to the Alamo, since the purpose of Fiesta was to honor the heroes of Texas' struggle for independence. Second, the Cavaliers would forever after select the King of Fiesta. Their third function would be to encourage close relations between San Antonio's civilian and military populations. There would be a fourth major project for the organization that would not come about until fifteen years later: the now famous River Parade.

According to Henry Graham, in his fascinating *History of the Texas Cavaliers*, published in 1976, Carrington had even bigger things in mind. He envisioned the Cavaliers as a statewide organization, headquartered in San Antonio but with chapters in many cities. They would meet annually in the Alamo City at Fiesta time.

Graham says that Carrington had still another purpose for the Cavaliers. After thirty-five years of growth, Fiesta had become a complex operation. By 1906, it had grown to a point that the women who started it, the Battle of Flowers Association, turned its direction over to a new Spring Festival Association. On May 26, 1913, this evolved into the Fiesta San Jacinto Association. Carrington, who had watched the celebration expand over two decades, was convinced that it needed better management. His belief was that the Cavaliers could help provide it.

In this sense, he was a seer. It would not happen for another thirty-three years, but eventually there would be dissension and disagreement within the Fiesta organization. In 1959 both the city government and the Chamber of Commerce stepped in to arbitrate. The result was the chartering of the Fiesta San Antonio Commission, still the official agency for the event. Ellis Shapiro, a New Jersey native who had moved to San Antonio in 1945 and opened a successful public relations practice, was named the first executive vice-president.

The establishment of this coordinating agency brought to fruition Carrington's dream for the celebration. It was a success from the outset, putting Fiesta on a sound financial footing, providing more organizations a role in making policy, and encouraging ever-growing participation by all segments of the population.

Along with Fiesta itself, the Cavaliers also had changed. In the beginning, Carrington demanded that the organization emphasize both horsemanship and medieval trappings — objectives with which some members neither agreed nor relished. Only twelve days after the founding of the order, he

sent his new "Knights" into combat and called the occasion a Tournament of Roses — the first of four that he would stage between 1926 and 1929.

For this first clash of arms, Carrington chose San Pedro Park at Myrtle and San Pedro and temporarily renamed it St. Peter's Wold ("wold" being an old English term for park). Most of his new Cavaliers were anything but expert horsemen, so he drafted many officers from Fort Sam Houston's Cavalry as "contestants."

A Knight in Old San Antone

In his history of the Cavaliers, Graham writes that the ceremony was as rigid as any combat between the Knights of King Charles I and the Roundheads who fought it out in England in 1642–1649. The Grand Marshal was instructed to make sure that the jousting was conducted "in strict, knightly form." It was.

A bugler called the combatants to action. As each Knight was announced, he rode his horse to the center of the field and saluted the dignitaries. In 1926 a King had not been selected. This was an oft-repeated oversight by Fiesta planners which Carrington would correct the next and succeeding years. However, Queen Agnes Terrell and her Court were present and took the bows. Each Knight then proceeded to the Duchess or other lady whom his anticipated victory would honor and knelt as she pinned a rose on his breast. Then he kissed her hand, mounted his horse, and entered the fray.

It was not a sham fight. The climax was a melee between twenty Knights. Ten, wearing red plumes on their rented helmets, represented the House of Lancaster. Ten foes representing the House of York had white plumes. Each carried a yardlong saber. The objective was to decapitate only the plume, not the head, of the opponent. Carrington, probably aware of his personal liability in the matter, had seen to it that both sides were heavily padded beneath their coats of mail and protected by masks.

However, he had not anticipated one technical problem. A Knight who had lost his plume and was thus legally "dead" under tournament rules could not see the top of his helmet. He went on fighting for his honor although the panel of distinguished judges (three generals from local army posts) tried to signal him of his demise.

The first King to be selected by the new Cavaliers was Sterling C. Burke, who assumed the throne as Antonio IX in 1927. He was clad in traditional royal robes, in keeping with the desires of Cavalier founder John Carrington, and his sixteen aides wore long tunics of chain mail. Neither the King nor his retinue liked the outfits, and before the 1928 Fiesta they switched to military uniforms similar to those worn in ceremonies today.

— *Fiesta San Antonio Commission*

Even Hollywood Came to Film the Show

The House of Lancaster won the most points and the tournament trophy. Top individual winner was "Sir" Harry Roper, dubbed a Knight of the Alamo for his good work. This act of bravery, however, did not ensure his election to the old, aristocratic Order of the Alamo. Its members felt that public jousting was beneath their dignity.

Whether it was dignified or not, this initial Tournament of Roses contributed another "first" to the history of Fiesta. Two newsreel companies had cameras trained on the action, and thousands of moviegoers saw the action later in theaters throughout the country.

Nevertheless, many of the Cavaliers did not aspire to star in newsreels, especially if they had to wear coats of mail and ride horses, and there was some internal quibbling over Carrington's ideas about what the members should wear in public and his insistence that they be horsemen. The latter objections were overcome some years later when the shortage of horses and riders made further tournaments and mounted parades impractical. The manner of Cavalier dress continued to be a point of contention with many, but not with Sterling Clinton Burke, the first King chosen by the organization.

Previous monarchs had always dressed in costumes they assumed were in the style of medieval kings. When Burke became King Antonio IX in 1927, he did not object to the traditional royal regalia. With his crown, he wore a trailing ermine cloak over a lace-trimmed tunic with knee britches and buckled shoes, and he carried a scepter. He looked like he had just walked off the stage of a Shakespearean drama, but he smilingly wore the outfit for all public appearances.

Who Said "Clothes Make the Man"?

Less gracious were the Cavaliers of lower royal rank. The sixteen who served as the King's escort were outfitted by Carrington in wine and tan hauberks, the long tunics of chain mail worn from the twelfth to the fourteenth century as defensive armor. Another tunic, this one of blue and gold and emblazoned with each Knight's coat of arms, was worn over the armor. Each also was fitted with a helmet, a surcoat, and a sword. Most resented of all were the black tights.

Even if the regalia had not made the Cavaliers look like extras off a movie set, the heat of a San Antonio spring made these outfits almost unbearable.

April temperatures can hover between 90 and 100 degrees and cause heat prostration even among the scantily dressed. There is no recorded incident of such casualties among the knightly Cavaliers, but even the official minutes of the organization indicate that there was deep resentment among the members forced to wear the armor.

Matters came to a head before the 1928 Tournament of Roses. A group of Cavaliers met for lunch at the Menger Hotel and unanimously agreed that the medieval dress had to go for comfort's sake. They voted for military-style uniforms of red and blue. Then, without further approval, they walked across Alamo Plaza to Frank Bros. Men's Store and ordered thirty-one uniforms from a mail order catalog. Each cost $37. A fancier outfit was ordered for the King for $70.

Legend has it (aided by frequent media misstatements) that the Cavalier uniform was designed to look like that of the French Foreign Legion, but spokesmen for the organization deny this. The colors — blue military jackets with notched lapels and red trousers — are similar. However, the original Cavalier uniform included a small-crowned Italian "bandman's" cap, a blue coat worn with a Sam Browne belt and saber, red riding britches with a blue stripe, black riding boots with spurs, and a *fourragere* worn around the left shoulder.

Napoleon's Best?

Although Carrington opposed discarding medieval dress for the Cavaliers, he was pleased that they added a *fourragere* to their new uniforms. This metal-tipped cord of colored braid originated with Napoleon Bonaparte as a unit citation for his troops. The combination of colors in the braid signified to the knowledgeable the honors bestowed on the unit. In choosing their *fourragere*, the Cavaliers, either by accident or intent, gave themselves an additional accolade.

The *fourragere* worn with the 1928 uniforms were black. Later red replaced the black for regular members and that of King Antonio was gold. The colored braid indicates that their unit has won six decorations, which in France would mean they had achieved the Legion of Honor. Napoleon also created the Legion, of course, to signify the special bravery of certain of his troops.

The Cavaliers retained the *fourragere* when they took a further step toward modern dress in 1941 and made slacks optional for those who opposed knee britches. Five years later, they copied the Air

In a solemn, rarely photographed ceremony, Ward Orsinger assumes the scepter of King Antonio XVI from his fellow Cavaliers in 1934.

— San Antonio Light *Collection,*
Institute of Texan Cultures

Force and adopted a sharply tailored coat with winged lapels. A broad-crowned cap replaced the Italian type.

Carrington, while he assented to the majority opinion in the matter of dress, continued to oppose the substitution of modern military uniforms for his beloved coats of mail. He never wore the uniform of the organization he founded, insisting that his short, stocky figure was the real reason.

Even some of the Cavaliers who wanted the new regalia were in for a surprise. Jack Ward Beretta, as Antonio XI in 1929, was the first King to wear a military uniform instead of an ermine robe. The new duds included the tall, plumed hat so familiar today to Fiesta-watchers. As the first King to ride in the Battle of Flowers Parade, he wore the outfit in public for the first time, but not without incident.

In 1983, when he was eighty-four, he recalled in an interview: "The parade went down through the Mexican part of town, and the people began to yell, *'Viva el gallo! Viva el gallo!'* They thought I was a rooster because I had a cap with plumes in it.''

The Cavaliers Make History in D.C.

No one would mistake the King for a rooster years later when the Cavaliers were invited to march in the inaugural parade of the new U.S. president, Gen. Dwight D. Eisenhower. Even in the nation's capital, the Cavalier uniform created a minor footnote to American history.

The incident happened in 1952. The Cavaliers arrived in Washington aboard a Katy Railroad special train on January 19. Among the contingent were seven prominent attorneys: Stanley Banks, John Bitter, Gilbert Denman, T. Maxey Hart, Lewis Kayton, Theo Weiss, and John H. Wood. Before the inaugural ceremonies the next day, the seven decided to add a unique item to their agenda for that historic occasion. They agreed to go as a group and seek admittance to practice before the Supreme Court of the United States.

Then, as now, the Court had an ironclad rule: only attorneys representing the military could appear before the bench in uniform. Others had to wear appropriate civilian clothes, meaning coats and ties for men. Unfortunately, the Cavaliers had planned that their uniforms would be their only dress and hadn't brought business suits along.

But even the Supreme Court can be overruled on some matters if one has enough influence. The Cavaliers did. After phone calls to congressmen and other well-placed officials from Texas, the Court permitted the Cavalier attorneys to appear in uniform. Chief Justice Fred Vinson presided, and the Court granted the San Antonians permission to practice before that august bench with one caveat: none of the seven could ever appear before the Court again in the uniform of a Cavalier!

They Liked Ike

Marching in an inaugural parade was not a new experience for the Cavaliers. In 1949 they had trekked to Washington by special train to march down Pennsylvania Avenue when Harry S Truman of Missouri was inaugurated for a full term. Four years later, the installation of a new president took on special significance.

Dwight D. Eisenhower was the first native Texan to assume the nation's highest office. Born October 14, 1890, in Denison, where his father was an engine wiper for the Katy Railroad, Ike had close ties to Texas. San Antonio had a special place in his heart. The love of his life began there.

On his graduation from West Point, his first assignment was to Fort Sam Houston. One morning in October 1915, he left the bachelor officers' quarters at the historic post. Sitting on the porch of the infantry officers' mess directly across the street was an old friend, Mrs. Lula Harris, wife of another Fort Sam officer. She had some guests and waved at young Eisenhower to come and meet them.

Her guests were a wealthy socialite family from Denver named Doud. They liked to spend their winters in San Antonio and lived in a house on McCullough not far from the army post. They had driven out to visit Mrs. Harris and had brought their daughter, Mamie, along. Young Ike was immediately attracted to Mamie. He was officer of the guard that day and invited her to walk his assignment with him that evening. She did.

He saw her again the next day and continued to see her almost daily for the rest of the winter. By Valentine's Day, they were engaged. In June they were married in Denver and he was made a first lieutenant the same day. After a brief honeymoon to Abilene, Kansas, where his family had moved from Denison, they returned to a two-room apartment at Fort Sam. There was born their first child, Doud David, who would die three years later of scarlet fever.

Throughout his army career, the Eisenhowers kept their tender memories of San Antonio, returning often. So when an invitation came to the Cavaliers to participate in his inauguration as president, it was accepted. For many, the journey was a sentimental one.

Sentiment always has played a role in Cavalier activities, a trait which historian Graham attributes to founder Carrington who, he writes, ''was, in the best sense of the word, a sentimental man. It was his sentiment — his sense of heritage, of legend, lore and pageantry — that infused the Cavaliers with the unique spirit that is their hallmark. And of all that has endured throughout their history, this is the Cavaliers' most substantial and valued tradition.''

7

The Kings

"If he be not fellow with the best king, thou shalt find him the best king of good fellows."
— **William Shakespeare,** *King Henry V*

In the beginning, there was King Cotton, followed by Selamat (tamales spelled backward) and Omala (Alamo backward), Zeus, and Rex. And sometimes there was no King at all on the Fiesta throne, even after Dr. Thomas Terrell Jackson, as Antonio I, began the dynasty which has endured since.

In the early days of the Battle of Flowers, choosing a King wasn't given a great deal of thought. Until 1926, when John B. Carrington founded the Cavaliers, there was no specific group that inquired into the lineage of those aspiring to Fiesta royalty. The first King, Alexander Y. Walton of San Antonio, was named in 1896 by the sponsors of a ball extolling cotton as a crop. Sharing the throne with Ida Archer of Austin, the controversial first Fiesta Queen, Walton was dubbed "King Cotton."

Next the Chamber of Commerce assumed the role of king-maker for a time and the throne went on the auction block. Any local man willing to contribute $1,500 or more could be almost certain of being anointed as Fiesta's monarch. Later the Fiesta San Jacinto Association and other groups named Kings. Today, however, only Antonio and El Rey Feo occupy Fiesta thrones. The Fiesta San Antonio Commission "froze" royalty at its present level so that there can never be any additional Kings or Queens in the celebration.

The oldest, most prestigious throne is still that of Antonio. As Fiesta celebrates its centennial in 1991, Antonio LXIX will reign — the sixty-ninth King in a dynasty that began in 1915.

Before the ascendancy of King Antonio, the Fiesta throne was not always occupied. In 1902 and 1903, there was neither a King nor a Queen, and no King in 1911. And there was no royalty during

World War I (Fiesta itself was canceled in 1918). Activities were resumed in 1919, but the King's throne was again vacant in 1925 and 1926.

It was during this period that somebody got their arithmetic mixed up and skipped an order of succession. Antonio IV had ruled in 1921, but somehow he was succeeded by Antonio VI. Antonio V simply got omitted and the error was never corrected. The last King who reigned before the Cavaliers took over the task of selecting that personage was Lt. Col. Charles R. Tips. He was called Antonio VIII, although he was only the seventh individual to hold that title.

In fact, the entire reign of the Antonios began in a unique way. It happened during the period when the throne was bought outright. Often friends would form a group, somewhat like a political fund-raising committee today, and raise the needed money to put a favorite in as ruler. Usually the organizers chose an exotic and fictitious name as they went about seeking contributions.

The King Named for a Saint

The one set up in behalf of Dr. Jackson was called the Gran Quivera, after the mythical land of golden cities that Spanish *conquistadores* came to Texas hoping to find. None of the legendary Seven Cities of Cibolo had been given names by those who swore they existed, but those in the Gran Quivera liked the name "San Antonio" and thought it should have been appropriate for a golden kingdom. If it was suitable for a saint (Anthony of Padua), it certainly would be for their Fiesta monarch. He was dubbed Antonio I.

Between 1915 and the organization of the Cavaliers in April 1926, there had been only eight An-

On April 22, 1913, King Rex (J. Bruce Martindale) arrives by special train at the Southern Pacific depot to assume his rule over Fiesta. The King is in the white ermine robe at right. Mayor Albert Steves delivers the formal welcome while county and city officials, hats off in respect, hail the new royalty.

— *Ann Russell Collection, Institute of Texan Cultures*

tonios on the Fiesta throne because of lapses in selecting them. When the Cavaliers were formed, the 1926 Fiesta was almost ready to begin and the throne remained vacant. Once the festivities ended, however, the job of choosing the 1927 King began. As one of their first official acts, the Cavaliers chose one of their own. The twenty-seven-year-old Sterling Burke was both single and the son of Jack Burke who, in 1921, had been Antonio VI. Young Burke became Antonio IX, continuing the dynasty established by the Gran Quivera.

"All aboard . . ."

In addition to carrying on the Antonio name, the Cavaliers wanted to follow another precedent for the royal entrance of their King into his realm. Since 1900, the King (when there had been one) arrived by train except for a couple of occasions when he entered via the river. For Antonio IX, the Cavaliers chartered a special train, put him aboard at a secret station east of the city, and had him arrive at exactly 7:50 P.M. on April 19, 1927, at the Southern Pacific depot on Commerce.

Awaiting him were the mayor, Fiesta Association officers, representatives of the military, a mounted escort of Cavaliers (they were still horsemen in those days), and even a band made up of railroad employees. As the train halted, whistles went off all over town. Loudest of these was at the nearby Alamo Iron Works. It was known locally as the "wildcat" because its shrill was reminiscent of the jungle beast. Julius Holmgren, founder of the company, had bought the monster in Chicago, and it had welcomed each Fiesta monarch from the beginning.

Almost at the moment the train stopped, a sudden rainstorm hit. It would last an hour. On board, the King Antonio, mindful of the expensive robes he wore, refused to get off. Eventually, aides persuaded him to exit, and he mounted his throne which had been placed atop a horse-drawn float. In this manner, he and his entourage proceeded to the Alamo. The rain had sent expected onlookers fleeing, and the formal welcoming program was scratched.

In early days of the Antonios, their ascension to the throne was with a good deal of pomp and occasional silliness. No more. Today a new King is installed in solemn ceremonies at the Alamo. He arrives in his carriage at the historic old mission at 6:45 P.M. on the opening Saturday of Fiesta. The Cavaliers file silently into the church. Candles are lit to honor the Alamo heroes and Cavalier dead, and a bugler plays taps. The outgoing King awards medals to his officers and proclaims new members by dubbing them on each shoulder with his sword as they kneel before him.

For Members Only

This part of the ceremony is restricted to Cavaliers only. Then the members file outside, where the public is gathered and where a twenty-one-gun salute announces the arrival of the new King in front of the Alamo. As fellow Cavaliers stand at attention with crossed swords, he walks to the old King and kneels. Antonio is not crowned. He is handed his plumed hat, saber, and medallion by his predecessor, and a key to the city by the mayor. He then turns to the crowd and says: "Let the merriment begin." Fiesta is then officially under way.

Although he arrived by carriage, the new King leaves the ceremony in a convertible with a police escort. This will be his transportation for much of Fiesta. The carriage, now used only for ceremonial occasions, will be the royal vehicle for the fifty-second time in 1991. It has a special history all its own.

The carriage was a gift in 1939 of George Friedrich, a Cavalier and San Antonio businessman. Those knowledgeable of such vehicles will recognize it as a C-spring Victoria, once popular with the elite in the pre-automobile era. Friedrich refurbished it in his plant and presented it to the organization. It was officially dedicated on April 11, 1939.

Six days later, it made its first official appearance when it took Antonio XXI, Dr. J. Layton Cochran, from the Missouri Pacific depot where he arrived by special train to the induction ceremonies at the Alamo.

During more than a half century of service, the carriage has appeared in each Battle of Flowers Parade as the King's official vehicle. It also has gone on many of the junkets the Cavaliers have made, among them the Eisenhower inauguration in 1953, the St. Paul Winter Carnival in 1955, and appearances at Dallas in Cotton Bowl parades.

Police Escorts and Borrowed Limousines

The carriage, of course, is now too old, too impractical in today's motorized world, and too valuable to use except on very special occasions. During the almost two weeks that Antonio spends visiting schools, hospitals, nursing homes, service clubs and

Above: Long before the Cavaliers began choosing their monarch in 1927, other Kings ruled Fiesta with pomp and circumstance. Here King Rex (J. Bruce Martindale) poses with his royal court on April 22, 1913.

— *Ann Russell Collection, Institute of Texan Cultures*

This flower-covered automobile and pretty occupant added glamour to the 1938 Battle of Flowers.

— San Antonio Light *Collection, Institute of Texan Cultures*

dozens of other spots, he travels in a white convertible loaned by friends or local automobile dealers. Usually his escort has been San Antonio police on motorcycles with sirens open and red lights blinking, but this has varied with the times.

Jack Beretta, who reigned as Antonio XI in 1929, was the first to be accorded this courtesy. In the 1950s, however, a few taxpayers objected, saying that such an escort was both expensive and in bad taste. The city government by ordinance stopped the practice.

In recent years, Antonio has had his escort returned, but it's not a public expense. The Cavaliers hire off-duty police to serve as the King's escort, but the city government still imposes one caveat. The royal entourage, including its motorcycle brigade with flashing red lights, cannot ignore the law. It must stop at all red traffic lights just as the peasants of the realm must.

Beretta's police escort is only one of the legacies he left to his successors. Another is what is known as the "King's visits."

When Antonio XI was on the throne, his schedule was not as proscribed as that of today's Fiesta monarch and often he had time on his hands. Beretta recounted to a reporter in 1983 how an endearing tradition was born: "We were staying at the St. Anthony Hotel, which was always the headquarters at that time of the Cavaliers," he recalled. "We were sitting around the hotel with nothing to do, so Bill King, one of my aides, said: 'Why don't we go out to Santa Rosa Hospital?' "

King's wife, Margaret, had just given birth to William, Jr., and the Cavaliers' King Antonio and his entourage paid the baby and his mother a visit. The nuns at the hospital, impressed with the group's French Foreign Legion-looking uniforms, asked them to tour the orphanages.

Thus began the King's Visits, an annual event that has seen Antonio greet youngsters not only in orphanages and hospitals, but also in schools throughout the city. Today the visits include nursing homes and other institutions. However, he no longer is the only royal personage to make such calls during Fiesta. Now there also is *El Rey Feo*, "The Ugly King."

The Coming of the Ugly King

His emergence from the rank of commoners in 1947 probably came as no surprise to either the Cavaliers or their Antonio. Even Shakespeare, who had a preoccupation about royalty in his plays, observed in *King Henry IV* that "uneasy is the head

that wears a crown." So it was that after Cotton, Selamat, Omala, and seventeen Cavalier Antonios, a second monarch appeared to threaten the old order.

His sponsors insisted that neither the realm of Antonio XXV or his successors would ever be endangered by the newcomer to the fantasyland of Fiesta San Antonio. They kept their promise. While there were some tensions between the two kingdoms early on, these were resolved. Now both have achieved separate but somewhat equal roles in the annual merriment.

The legend of the Ugly King dates back to medieval times in Spain. It seems that the king who sat on the Spanish throne had distanced himself from his subjects, filling his Court with only the rich and aristocratic. The ordinary taxpayer was not on any palace invitation list and rarely even saw the monarch except when he rode off to hunt with a coterie of "beautiful people," as the peasants called them. The common folk resented this, and a crowd gathered in the plaza one day and proclaimed one of their own as king.

Since the mob had no "beautiful people" among its members, they dubbed their chosen ruler El Rey Feo, "The Ugly King."

Some of this same sentiment existed in 1947. There were thousands of San Antonians who, while they loved the fun of Fiesta, felt that it was created and run by the city's old, moneyed, aristocratic families. There was little public expression of resentment, but it did exist. And many among the city's ever-growing Hispanic population remembered, or had heard of, a celebration in the village of Aguascalientes, Mexico, on St. Mark's Day called *La Feria de San Marcos*. It was ruled by a Rey Feo.

Members of Council No. 2 of the League of United Latin American Citizens (LULAC) knew of La Feria de San Marcos when they were looking for a way to raise money to provide scholarships for worthy Hispanics. They decided it would be practical — and also a little fun — if they sponsored a celebration of their own and picked an Ugly King to reign opposite Antonio. They called it *La Feria de las Flores* (the Fair of the Flowers) and chose both a King and a Queen.

A Monarch That Raises Money

In the beginning, the LULAC sponsors made it clear that their selection of a King would be "inclusive rather than exclusive" — an obvious barb at

The King's carriage is almost as much a Fiesta tradition as Antonio himself. The English-style vehicle was purchased in Montreal, Canada, and made its first appearance in the Battle of Flowers on April 17, 1939, when it carried Antonio XXI, Dr. Layton Cochran. It was making its eighteenth appearance in this 1957 photo when Antonio XXXV, Ames Gill, was beginning his reign.

       — *Zintgraff Collection, Institute of Texan Cultures*

the Cavaliers' tradition of always choosing one of their own. Also, El Rey Feo's principal function would be fund-raising, and his selection would depend entirely on how much money he could put into LULAC's coffers by selling votes to his friends. To make sure that he would have this ability, LULAC has never opened the election to just any candidate.

Each year, the Scholarship Committee reviews a list of nominees, both Anglo and Hispanic. Its first requirement is a name that is well known to the community. Next it looks for a record of involvement in civic affairs. If the individual also has

Jack Beretta, Antonio XI in 1919, was the first King to make regular visits to hospitals during his reign. He is shown here at a Texas Cavalier party during Fiesta 1939.

— San Antonio Light *Collection, Institute of Texan Cultures*

raised funds for his church or some other worthy cause, he can almost be certain of nomination.

Votes for the election of the first El Rey Feo went for only a penny each, and early Ugly Kings were lucky if they could sweeten the scholarship pot by $3,000. Now it is not unusual for a Rey Feo to add as much as $100,000 to the program, and he collects more dollars now than many of his predecessors did pennies.

Despite his worthy objectives, the Ugly King was regarded for thirty-two years by Fiesta planners as a somewhat comic figure that was colorful but had no real role in the celebration. And there was some resentment among the old aristocracy at what they perceived to be an invasion of the realm of the true Fiesta monarch. Some objected to the fact that this upstart King bought his throne with cash contributed by himself and friends. That this money went for a laudable cause was not enough to soothe the nay-sayers. Money had never been involved, even covertly, in the selection of King Antonio. Since 1927, he has been elected in a secret ballot cast by his fellow Cavaliers — the exclusive organization in which membership is a pedigree guaranteeing a royal status acceptable to San Antonio society.

Thus upgrading the status of El Rey Feo, especially in areas where King Antonio had reigned supreme for so long, required careful diplomacy on the part of both monarchies. Fortunately, the protocol was handled correctly in all cases and El Rey Feo was formally invited to be a part of Fiesta in 1980 and given his own parade.

Apparently, the dual reign of Antonio and El Rey Feo satisfies the need for masculine royalty at Fiesta. No other kings have appeared to contest their thrones. However, in 1987, merchants along the River Walk decided to have their own festival each January as a business promotion at a time when tourists are sparse. They call their show the annual River Bottom Festival and elect a Mud King and Queen. It's another case of the occupants buying their earthly tiaras by urging their friends to "sling mud" (pronounce that "money") at their campaign. Votes, at a nickel each, raise several thousands of dollars each year for the Paseo del Rio Association. This event has no connection with the Fiesta San Antonio Commission.

Meanwhile, the emergence of the two major Fiesta Kings has, in the words of one Anglo who served as El Rey Feo, "built a bridge between both" of the city's major cultures. Both monarchs now make royal visits around town, often traveling

Logan Stewart, in the white uniform, was the first Ugly King to ride in an El Rey Feo Parade. Here he and Ricks Wilson, King Antonio LVIII, exchange toasts to signal the beginning of a cooperative effort between their two kingdoms for the future benefit of Fiesta. Thad M. Ziegler, center, a former president of the Fiesta San Antonio Commission, would become Antonio LXVI eight years later.

— Parrish Photography

together. Each King honors his counterpart with a party, and in recent years, each has conferred his organization's highest award on the other.

The Red Plume and the Cabrito

Like so many other facets of Fiesta, these awards are unique. King Antonio, because he wears a tall cap with a red plume instead of a crown, long ago formed the Order of the Red Plume. Members are former Antonios. Now, how-ever, the reigning Antonio inducts the Ugly King into the order also.

El Rey Feo returns the favor by making Anto-nio a member of the Order of the Cabrito. *Cabrito* is Spanish for "little goat," and tradition has it that the legendary El Rey Feo was presented one by his loyal subjects as a gesture of ridicule to the real King. The first Ugly King crowned by LULAC also was given a live goat, and the practice has con-tinued. Today the presentation is considered a signal honor, and so El Rey Feo created his Order of the Cabrito as a special award that only he can confer.

8

Here Come the Bands

*"You won't do any business, if you haven't got a band:
The folks expect a street parade and uniforms so grand."*
— **George M. Cohan**

In Meredith Wilson's hit show *The Music Man*, it took seventy-six trombones leading the big parade to inspire the residents of his mythical River City.

Not so in San Antonio, where parade watching approaches an art form. In most years, the Alamo City will average a parade a week. And during Fiesta, the number jumps to three major ones in ten days and at least that many smaller neighborhood processionals.

Fiesta always opens officially at 10:00 A.M. on the Friday before San Jacinto Day (April 21) with ceremonies in front of the Alamo. At 6:30 P.M. the first marchers take to the streets in a local shopping mall when the Girl Scouts field a miniscule parade in which the homemade floats are constructed primarily of shoeboxes.

Except for some impromptu sidewalk appearances by *mariachis* and other strolling street bands, the city is without another parade until the following Monday, when the Cavaliers' River Parade gets Fiesta off to a floating start and introduces King Antonio to his subjects.

The oldest and best-known — the Battle of Flowers — is the following Friday afternoon. Its elaborate, flower-bedecked floats are used to introduce the Queen, Princess, and the rest of her Court to the multitudes while dozens of marching bands provide the music. Although it's the Queen's parade, King Antonio rides along in his regal horse-drawn carriage.

The third featured parade, the night extravaganza known as Fiesta Flambeau, climaxes the celebration Saturday evening.

If these don't satisfy the voracious appetite of San Antonians and Fiesta guests for parades, there

are others. The King William Historic District opens its fair and tour of homes with a processional through the neighborhood. The famed Night in Old San Antonio begins its four-night stand with a parade in La Villita.

Even in San Antonio, however, not quite everybody loves a parade. Although the Battle of Flowers has almost achieved the status of a legal holiday, it doesn't monopolize the attention of all who throng Alamo Plaza and the main streets. Several other Fiesta events don't even pause for what has been acclaimed one of the nation's best street parades. Fiesta en la Villa de San Fernando opens two hours before the Flowers floats start their route, and Fiesta del Mercado opens at twelve noon sharp.

While the Cavaliers' River Parade may draw a quarter of a million to cheer the elaborate barges, thousands more ignore it to attend the Jaycees' La Semana Alegre music, food, and beer fest less than a quarter of a mile away. La Semana has one of its most successful nights at the same time the Fiesta Flambeau is lighting the city's heart with its two-and-a-half-hour parade.

However, there were still some who felt that a fourth was needed. Enter a new Rey Feo who decided he wanted to put his own procession on the street.

Two Kings on Parade

Since the election of the first El Rey Feo, the occupant of this throne often has been an Anglo. This was the case in 1979 when Logan Stewart, a popular local radio personality, raised the most funds for the League of United Latin American Cit-

Governor Dolph Briscoe, honorary grand marshal of the 1978 Battle of Flowers Parade, waves to the crowd.
— *Courtesy Elicson Photography, Blanco*

izens and was accorded the honor. For weeks before, Stewart had opened his daily newscasts by criticizing the Hispanics for not seeking a more active involvement in Fiesta. When he was chosen as El Rey Feo in August 1979, he decided it was his responsibility to take the initiative. He wanted to give the Ugly King more visibility by having his own parade.

Davis Burnett, executive vice-president of what was then the Fiesta San Antonio Association, was an ally. He invited Stewart and LULAC President Ray Doria to lunch where, for the first time, the idea of a parade for the Ugly King was discussed. Burnett urged them to apply to the commission for a permit. As a prelude to this action, however, they held meetings with both the Battle of Flowers Association and the Cavaliers — the two organizations whose votes on the commission could deny their request.

Approval by the directors of the Battle of Flowers came almost routinely. The Cavaliers required more convincing. Understandably, they feared that an El Rey Feo Parade would undermine the throne of their own Antonio. His status already had been diminished somewhat by the ruling of the Fiesta Commission that neither the Cavalier King nor the Order of the Alamo Queen were "official royalty" and had encouraged other groups to elect their own monarchs. Several Fiesta organizations had done just that, and the 1979 celebration had a bevy of Queens. No new Kings had come forth to challenge the realms of either Antonio or Rey Feo, and the general feeling seemed to be that a parade for the Ugly King would only add another dimension to Fiesta.

When LULAC's application for a Fiesta parade permit in the 1980 celebration reached the commission, it was approved without objection. However, the first march of the Ugly King was not memorable. The fancy, expensive floats had been committed, as always, to the Battle of Flowers. Almost every band in town had been signed by either that group or Fiesta Flambeau. But Stewart, using his new recognition as a Rey Feo of action, cajoled enough out-of-town music groups, army units, and decorated pick-up trucks to give him 116 entries. The production was a far cry from the Philadelphia Mummer's Parade or that of the Veiled Prophet in St. Louis, but it was destined to change the face of Fiesta San Antonio forever.

Most of the entries were pick-up trucks pulling flat-bed trailers that sponsors had decorated using nothing more than crepe paper and identifying signs. The bands were mostly imported from out of town; the Battle of Flowers and Fiesta Flambeau already had signed all but four of the San Antonio schools.

The military, however, responded to Rey Feo's pleas and the National Guard supplied some tanks and troop carriers. For a beginning, it was a respectable effort to stage a parade for the common people.

The El Rey Feo Parade continued through 1986, but it never reached the status of the Battle of Flowers, Flambeau, and the River Parades as an attraction. However, the Ugly King meanwhile had won the hearts of San Antonio and was sharing in many of the events that had once been the province only of the Cavaliers' Antonio. In 1987, when the Junior Chamber of Commerce gave up its sponsorship of Flambeau, the Fiesta San Antonio Commission asked LULAC and the Rey Feo to take over.

The King Without a Parade

The new relationship didn't last. As detailed in a later chapter, the League of United Latin American Citizens got into an internal dispute over the handling of Flambeau finances. When the national organization demanded that the Fiesta Commission remove LULAC Council No. 2 as sponsors of Flambeau and give the parade to the parent organization, the commission responded by forming a Fiesta Flambeau Association to take over sponsorship of the night parade. El Rey Feo no longer has his own procession.

However, the Ugly King may be more on parade now than ever before. He is in the River Parade with King Antonio and the old Fiesta royalty. He marches with the procession that opens A Night in Old San Antonio. In fact, he has become a part of just about every Fiesta event, including being an honored guest at the Coronation. As a result, San Antonians, including Hispanics, Anglos, and other ethnic groups, cheer both monarchs with equal fervor.

A Love-Hate Affair with Businesses

Although the three major Fiesta parades together bring out close to one million viewers and a television audience of thousands more, they are a love-hate proposition with San Antonio businesses. Most, though not all, close during the marches, but some resent the fact that they have no choice.

This is true of the several automobile dealers along North Broadway. While they applaud Fiesta

The Battle of Flowers Association Parade always brings out celebrities. Lady Bird Johnson, flanked by 5th Army commander Gen. Allen Burdette (left) and Jack Lewis (King Antonio LXI), wait in the reviewing stand for the start of festivities at the 1984 Fiesta San Antonio.

— *Fiesta San Antonio Commission*

as a bonanza for the city as a whole, they admit that it is a problem for them. By Thursday, before the Battle of Flowers Parade the next day and Fiesta Flambeau on Saturday night, they have all of their cars towed away and stored to protect them from damage by the crowds. Days before the weekend parades start, police erect barricades and bleacher seats are put in place. This discourages customers at a time when more than the usual numbers of potential buyers are in the area.

On the other hand, hotel and restaurant operators regard Fiesta as a gift from the gods. Hotel rooms are booked solid weeks and even months in advance, and it's a rare restaurant that doesn't have a line of hungry guests waiting for seating. The popularity of Fiesta (and of San Antonio as a convention and tourist center) long has provided local inns with the highest occupancy rate in the state.

Among the happiest of the business community are the float-builders. Most of the floats are designed and built by local professionals. One has been building many of the entries since 1975. He and the others begin their work six to seven months before Fiesta, when sponsors submit their themes for each float.

If the floats are to be self-propelled (and most are), they are built on automobiles that have had their roofs and sides removed. A framework of quarter-inch steel rods then is welded to the chassis. The design is constructed from plywood and chicken wire and then covered with plastic sheeting and flowers. An average float costs at least $5,000 to build and the more elaborate ones cost $25,000 and more.

Most are used only once, a few are sent to join parades in other cities, and some make four or five other parades before they are retired or rebuilt.

Homemade Floats at Fiesta? Incredible!

Not all are produced by professionals, however. For more than twenty years, students at St. George Episcopal Day School have, with the help of their parents and teachers, built their own float for the Battle of Flowers Parade. Each fall, a theme is selected and the work begins in an abandoned warehouse. The project includes much more than the construction and equipping of the float. The theme is used as a teaching unit throughout the school term.

One year the second-grade children, ages

The military has had a part in Fiesta since the first Battle of Flowers in 1891. In the 1917 parade, Gen. John J. Pershing, far right in the campaign hat, was a participant. He would leave San Antonio shortly afterward to become general of the armies and commander in chief of the American Expeditionary Forces in World War I.

— Ann Russell Collection, Institute of Texan Cultures

seven to eight, selected Southwestern Indians as the theme. Throughout the fall, the students studied Indian lore. Six weeks before Fiesta, students, teachers, and parents began the long job of building the float. Mothers made all of the colorful costumes and decorations for the float while the fathers wired and framed it. They even devised a machine so the students could send smoke signals to other tribes as they rode down Houston Street.

When completed, the St. George float compared favorably with those made by professionals. The students, each in Indian costume, wove baskets, ground corn, beat drums, and even scraped a buffalo skin as the parade moved along. Their float included an authentic reproduction of a tepee, a totem pole, and other artifacts that made it look as if it had been lifted from Yanaguana, the Indian village that once stood where the Alamo and La Villita are today.

Super Scoopers and Other Clean-up Efforts

Volunteer efforts like this are credited by many with allowing Fiesta to survive and grow over a century. Another group that made a unique contribution was students from Alamo Heights High School. Since 1961, these "Super Scoopers," as they call

themselves, have been cleaning up after the horses in every Fiesta parade. Armed with litter bags and scoops, a platoon of students follows each unit that includes horses. At the conclusion of the parades, the streets are virtually spotless.

Cleaning up the other litter following three major parades is a task requiring much time and manpower. It is a chore and an expense, however, to which San Antonians have never objected. Not only are the parades a major focus of Fiesta, but they have had a role in changing the very fabric of the city.

Over One Billion Entertained

It was the Battle of Flowers, which was planned as a one-time event originally, that gave birth to Fiesta. It was the River Parade and the magnificent Flambeau that helped make the event the ten-day extravaganza it is today. The Ugly King Parade of 1980, although of only short duration, also played an important part in the development of the celebration. By focusing on the interests of the predominant Hispanic population and the so-called "common people," it enlarged and solidified participation in Fiesta, making it truly everybody's jubilee.

Since 1891, it is estimated that well over a billion people have watched Fiesta parades. As might be expected, there are always some minor mishaps when as many as 500,000 gather in one area for one of these events. Only once in a century, however, has there been an occasion serious enough to cause cancellation of a parade.

The Day Nobody Cheered

Friday, April 27, 1979, is still remembered in San Antonio as "the day nobody cheered." What had started as another Battle of Flowers Parade became a time of death and terror. As one newspaper put it: "There were no villains that day. Only victims."

That fateful Friday dawned sunny and almost cloudless. At parade time, the temperature was in the low seventies. The crowds had started gathering early, many bringing along folding chairs and picnic lunches while they awaited the start of Fiesta's oldest parade. The Battle of Flowers had always represented San Antonio's best. The Queen of Fiesta, resting on her throne built atop a lavish float, soon would pass and wave at her loyal subjects. As it had for eighty-eight years, the pageantry of this parade was a magnet that had drawn a multitude to enjoy its fantasy.

Hundreds of these thousands had gathered at the intersection of Broadway and East Grayson, the assembly point for the parade units. Included was Ira Attebury, sixty-four, who liked to grow roses and who had brought his motor home down early and parked it in the lot of a tire store on the west side of Broadway. Then, at exactly 1:02 P.M., just as the first units of the parade were forming, Attebury opened the door of his recreational vehicle, pointed an AR-15 automatic weapon at the crowd, and began firing. When the gun jammed, he picked up two shotguns and fired more shots. Then he retreated inside and slammed the door.

When the barrage ended, two were dead. Among the fifty-five wounded were thirteen children and six policemen. Attebury had often told others that he feared and hated the police. His brief reign of terror cured that fear. Later, when officers broke into the motor home, Attebury was dead. He had shot himself in the temple.

It was, somebody said, "San Antonio's blackest day since the fall of the Alamo."

The Battle of Flowers was canceled immediately. It was the only time, except for the war years, that the parade has not been held.

9

When the River Becomes a Stage

"Time is a sort of river of passing events, and strong is its current; no sooner is a thing brought to sight than it is swept by and another takes its place, and this too will be swept away."
— **Marcus Aurelius Antoninus** (A.D. 121–180)

Robert H. H. Hugman was never a Cavalier nor a member of the Order of the Alamo. His name is not well known even today in the city where he made a municipal treasure out of a a dirty, sluggish stream. If it weren't for Hugman's vision, today's River Parade would not be one of the highlights of Fiesta.

In fact, there wouldn't even be a river bisecting the heart of San Antonio, creating an urban oasis that annually attracts more than three million visitors, including more than 250,000 for a single event: the Texas Cavaliers' River Parade.

Hugman was a young architect in 1919 when he first suggested that the little spring-fed river might one day attract tourists. Downtown merchants hooted at the idea. They wanted the channel filled in to stop the occasional flooding of their stores. Also, they argued that the space could better be used for parking cars, or the building of more shops.

Hugman, however, continued to dream. He believed the river could have the same appeal as the Seine in Paris, the Thames in London, or the Grand Canal of Venice. He drew up a set of plans for what he called "The Shops of Aragon and Romula." His proposal called for stores, restaurants, hotels, and landscaped "relaxation points" with Venice-like gondolas transporting shoppers, diners, tourists, and those just wanting to listen to the sounds of the outdoors.

Although they were never built as Hugman planned them, the Shops of Aragon and Romula captured the imagination of fifteen prominent women (including several who were wives of the businessmen who opposed the development). Four years earlier, they had organized as the San Anto-

nio Conservation Society. It would be the results of their efforts, along with help from the late congressman and mayor, Maury Maverick, Sr., and a handful of others that would save the river.

The Goose That Saved the River

The women developed a puppet show based on a nursery rhyme as their most telling argument. They marched into the City Council meeting and used their homemade puppets to show how paving the river would kill the goose that lays the golden egg. The men capitulated, and what is today one of San Antonio's favorite areas began to emerge.

Even before the construction of the Arneson River Theater and the beautification of the area, the stream had played a role in Fiesta. In 1905, King Selamat I had made his official entrance to the event via the river. Two years later, Selamat III had followed suit. The 1907 arrival had been planned to involve considerable pomp. Styled as a "Venetian Carnival," its parade of barges carried figures representing history, allegory, and myth. The King's boat was an elaborate "barge of state."

Best-laid plans often go awry, especially in the unpredictable weather of a San Antonio spring. To raise the water level to accommodate the barges, an earthen dam was hurriedly put in place so the armada could sail from the Houston Street bridge to the Carnegie Library. A sudden downpour fell just before the parade was to start, washing out the dam and demolishing some of the floats. The parade was canceled, the dam reconstructed, the barges repaired, and the first major River Parade came off two days later.

It was to be another quarter of a century, how-

Robert H. H. Hugman, the young architect who, in 1919, dreamed of making a municipal treasure out of a dirty, sluggish stream. Hugman finally convinced San Antonio businessmen that the river could have the same appeal as the Seine in Paris, the Thames in London and the Grand Canal in Venice.

— Portrait by Lewison Studio. Permission of Mrs. Robert H. H. Hugman.
From the Institute of Texan Cultures Collection

Mishaps like this one are common when barges take to the San Antonio River for the big water parade.

— *Fiesta San Antonio Commission*

ever, before Fiesta planners began to utilize the river fully in the annual celebration. Not until the late 1930s, when much of the beautification was complete, was the stream given a real role in Fiesta. The San Antonio Conservation Society began staging River Festivals then that were the origin of today's Night in Old San Antonio (see Chapter 11).

By 1940, with the river redevelopment nearing completion, it was decided that a parade would be an ideal way to show off what miracles good planning, hard work, and federal dollars can produce. The vehicle that appeared to the Texas Cavaliers as the best for this purpose was their own King's Entry into his realm. Not everybody agreed.

The Kings Trade the Train for a Barge

For reasons never made clear, the Fiesta San Jacinto Association (the predecessor organization that once ran the event) proposed that the King's Entry be changed. Instead of arriving by train as most monarchs had done, the Fiesta planners suggested that this event be combined with the pilgrimage to the Alamo — an idea with which the Cavaliers did not agree. Earlier William C. King,

as Antonio XIII, had suggested that His Royal Highness make his official entry by boat. When Mayor Maury Maverick, Sr., offered the Cavaliers the exclusive use of the Arneson River Theater for their event, they accepted.

Thus in 1941 the River Parade became the event that formally dedicated the beautification project.

It was not an easy task. Start-up costs were a problem. To get the money to build fifty *lanchas* (Spanish for launch or boat), San Antonio businessmen were asked to contribute $60 each. To the fifty-one who responded, the Cavaliers bestowed the rank of "Admirals of the San Antonio Navy."

Fifty of the six-by-twenty-foot plywood vessels with reinforced bottoms were built by Works Progress Administration workers. Without motors, they were propelled by poles and oars. Two-thirds of the fleet went to schools, the army, city officials, civic organizations, a business — anybody willing to build a float on them. The Cavaliers used the remainder, including a special barge for King Antonio.

The King's barge was designed to be the flagship. It was a contribution of George Friedrich,

Above: The river always has been the heart of San Antonio. Before the Texas Cavaliers first staged a River Parade in 1940 to introduce King Antonio to his subjects, the stream had been the site of an annual river pageant, as shown in this 1930s picture. It consisted mostly of decorated canoes and food booths along both banks.

— *San Antonio Museum Association*

Left: A star-studded cast of World War II heroes was featured in the 1948 River Parade. In the foreground, Gen. Walter Krueger is taking a seat on the VIP barge. Behind him, left to right, is an unidentified naval officer; Adm. Chester W. Nimitz, the Fredericksburg native who commanded the Pacific Fleet on its way to victory; and Gen. Jonathan M. Wainwright, hero of the Pacific war who later retired in San Antonio.

— San Antonio Light *Collection, Institute of Texan Cultures*

Not every gondola in Fiesta parades gets onto the river.
This one, an entry in the High School Queen's section in
the 1920s, was pulled by a horse in the Battle of Flowers.
— *San Antonio Museum Association*

In 1936, to help win support for plans to beautify the San Antonio River, Jack White, operator of the Plaza Hotel, and the Mexican Businessmen's Association joined to present a "Venetian Night" on the stream. This consisted of eighteen boats filled with Mexican children who later performed on the river bank.

— San Antonio Light *Collection,*
Institute of Texan Cultures

who had it specially constructed in his company's shops. Instead of plywood, the King's *lancha* was made of galvanized iron. The other barges, even with reinforced bottoms, were so fragile that someone jumping into one could have gone straight through to the water. Friedrich designed the King's barge "strong enough to withstand a torpedo." He didn't know it at the time, but he was destined to be the first to use it as Cavalier King Antonio XXIII.

When Antonio and his procession of barges sailed the river in that first parade, they were greeted by a hard rain shower. Nobody seemed to mind, however, and some 50,000 spectators lined the river, paying twenty cents for adults and a dime for children. It was, by contemporary accounts, an outstanding success.

The War Torpedoes the Show

Less than eight months after the Cavaliers inaugurated the River Parade, Japan bombed Pearl Harbor and the U.S. was at war. More than three-quarters of the members were to serve in some branch of the armed services. The rest soon became involved in nonmilitary roles. As had happened in World War I, all Fiesta activities were suspended for the duration.

On September 2, 1945, the Japanese signed the

Barges in the River Parade being placed by a crane into the San Antonio River. Days of decorating will follow before they make their appearance before the thousands who converge all along the river.

— San Antonio Light *Collection,*
Institute of Texan Cultures

formal surrender aboard the USS *Missouri*. Accepting it was Fleet Admiral Chester W. Nimitz, the Fredericksburg native who often said, "You can take the boy out of Texas, but you can't take Texas out of the boy." Three years later, he was back in Texas to ride in the Cavaliers' River Parade of 1948. All Fiesta events had been resumed in April 1946, and the first postwar River Parade was one of the premier events.

Meanwhile, the face of Fiesta had undergone subtle change. The gasoline engine had replaced the horse as power for the Battle of Flowers Parade floats. In fact, horses for ceremonial purposes were becoming hard to come by in a state that once prided itself on the fact that its equine population outnumbered people. By 1951, the Cavaliers, founded as a mounted troop, had trouble finding enough horses to provide the King's traditional guard for the Battle of Flowers. That would be the last year that the organization would ride instead of march.

Rough Waves on the River

Finding horses was not the only problem facing the Cavaliers. Funding the River Parade was another. Since the beginning, the organization had assumed the responsibility for all costs associated with that event, and these grew each year. Ticket sales to those viewing the parade and the sponsorship of floats by businesses helped, but individual members had to ante up additional funds each year to keep the parade going. In 1951 the Fiesta San Jacinto Association agreed to finance the River Parade, but with some caveats.

The event still would feature King Antonio, but the Fiesta bosses would call the shots. Soon the discontent sown by this new arrangement began to surface. Although the Fiesta San Jacinto Association was bankrolling the event, the Cavaliers still

considered it to be "their" parade. When the association began using the show to highlight its own "Miss Fiesta," the Cavaliers felt that it was an encroachment on the royal status of their King Antonio.

Friction and resentment grew on both sides. After the 1958 Fiesta, the Cavaliers decided to find a better way to bring Antonio into his mythical kingdom. There were several alternatives. One was to suggest to the Order of the Alamo a joint Coronation of their Queen and the Cavalier King. The idea had been summarily rejected by the Queen-makers before. There also was the possibility of bringing Antonio in by royal train, the mode of entry of earlier kings. A third option was to explore again the sponsorship of the River Parade by the Cavaliers.

No final decision was reached. But in 1959, the King made his official entry in a colorful ceremony at the Alamo rather than the River Parade. This, in effect, was a snub at the Fiesta San Jacinto Association. The Cavaliers' action was applauded by other participating organizations which also had become dissatisfied with the manner in which the association was operating Fiesta. When the Cavaliers voted to resign from that organization, powerful groups like the Battle of Flowers, the Conservation Society, the Order of the Alamo, and others followed suit.

Concerned about the future of Fiesta, the Chamber of Commerce and city officials stepped in. A new Fiesta San Antonio Commission was formed and one of its first acts was to return the River Parade to the Cavaliers. The Junior Chamber of Commerce became a co-sponsor.

Co-sponsorship of the River Parade with the Jaycees continued until 1968. Under the arrangement, the Junior Chamber had charge of ticket sales and seating, but the Cavaliers were solely responsible for staging the event. Now the parade is the exclusive project again of the Cavaliers.

10

A Thousand Points of Light

"There are two ways of spreading light; to be the candle, or the mirror that reflects it."
— **Edith Wharton**

It has been called "America's largest illuminated night parade." The millions who have watched it light the way to the final weekend of the feasting and frolicking that is Fiesta say that it is also the best.

The idea of a lighted parade, now one of the premier events of Fiesta, was the brainchild of a civil engineer named Reynolds Andricks. In 1948 he was elected to the board of the old Fiesta San Jacinto Association despite his warnings that he knew nothing about parades, floats, and marching bands and could not care less about them. Later he would recall his first meeting as a board member this way: "I was astounded that so few people seemed interested in Fiesta. They didn't think that they had enough events to attract visitors for at least a week. I argued that they should add another parade and that it should be at night." He called it "Fiesta Flambeau."

Flambeau is a French word that literally means a tall, decorated candlestick or a burning torch. Marchers in San Antonio's Fiesta Flambeau Parade have used both, plus individual flashlights on occasion, to give the cool Texas evening the appearance of being illuminated by thousands of stars.

The idea wasn't entirely original with Andricks. He had watched night parades at New Orleans' Mardi Gras. But he believed that he could create one that was unique.

He needed help, however, and knew where to find it. At Fredericksburg, the German community in the Hill Country seventy-five miles west of San Antonio, William (Bill) Petmecky lived a double life. For years he was the tax assessor-collector for Gillespie County and later was the Fredericksburg postmaster. But for half a century, he also had been active in county fairs and was recognized as a festi-val impressario.

Petmecky had started the famed Easter Fires Pageant in Fredericksburg, writing the script and a booklet about the legend. By the time Andricks was planning Fiesta Flambeau, Petmecky had become nationally known as a creator of folk festivals. He was delighted to have a part in planning Fiesta's first illuminated night parade.

Literally Giving Flambeau a "Flare"

The two planners decided that the most effective way to light the line of march was to have torch brigades made up of four men each. They would march at intervals between each ten units, carrying flares like those used by police and truckers as warning devices at accident scenes. Each torch would be attached to a five-foot pole. Bands would attach flashlights to their music stands, and floats would be lighted in whatever unique way the designers might think up. The idea (forty years before President George Bush mentioned it in a speech) would be to provide a thousand, or more, points of light.

The association approved his plan, but Andricks faced the problem of where to find participants. The Battle of Flowers had been going on for fifty-seven years, and its parade had a national reputation. Its sponsors already had arranged for beautiful floats and signed the best bands. However, Andricks noted that the military was not entering floats in the parade. To enlist the participation of this huge segment of San Antonio's population, he started with a call on the commanding general of Fort Sam Houston and then went to each air base commander.

In each case, the military brass liked the idea.

71

This traditional float was used by Miss Fiesta for many years in the Fiesta Flambeau.

— *Zintgraff Collection, Institute of Texan Cultures*

Every entry in the Fiesta Flambeau Parade has to light its own way. Kerosene torches were used for many years and reintroduced in 1990.

— San Antonio Light *Collection, Institute of Texan Cultures*

King Antonio takes part in all parades, but in the Fiesta Flambeau, the royal driver dims the headlights on the King's convertible. His Royal Highness doesn't want to outshine other entries in the famous night parade.

— *Zintgraff Collection, Institute of Texan Cultures*

Andricks made his proposal more enticing by suggesting that each base elect its own Queen and have her ride its float. This was a startling proposal since many might think that the military beauties would be competing with the throne of the Order of the Alamo Queen. Andricks assured them that Fiesta had grown large enough to accommodate some additional crowned heads. He also made it clear that he was establishing a new line of nobility that would be known only as Flambeau Royalty.

Crowding the Royal Realm

The announcement that some new sovereigns would have a role in Fiesta came as a surprise to the the Order of the Alamo and the Texas Cavaliers, heretofore the sole creators of royalty. Nevertheless, Andricks went ahead with his plans and the first Flambeau boasted a half dozen military bands and a similar number of floats, each adorned by a Queen. Today the military nobility is an accepted and appreciated part of Fiesta.

Andricks, however, didn't want his parade to look like troops marching to war. Never one to stand on protocol, he turned next to groups that previously had been either overlooked accidentally or ignored deliberately by what he called "the high society" sponsors of the Battle of Flowers and River parades. He wanted color and variety, and he got it.

First, the Shriners came in with their fez-topped band and a group of their famed trick cyclists. Next he solicited commercial firms to join; they could afford fancy floats like those in the Battle of Flowers, and he convinced them that such visibility would be good for business. Soon civic clubs and social groups became a part of Flambeau.

The latter additions were particularly intrigued, Andricks said later, by his idea to stage "a parade of nations section where Americans who have pride in their heritage have an opportunity to build a float emblematic of their country."

At meetings of the Fiesta San Jacinto Association, Andricks had also expressed concern that the other two Fiesta parades were too parochial. Other communities for years had sent Duchesses to the Coronation of the Queen, but the floats in her Battle of Flowers Parade were purely local. Andricks decided to take his cause to the hinterlands.

"Come one, come all..."

"I visited festivals throughout South Texas and made deals with them," he told a reporter. "If they'd send a float to Flambeau, I'd send a float to their parade."

It worked. Within a year or two, there were as many as twenty-five out-of-town floats following torch-bearers in the Flambeau. Andricks was elated.

This "exchange program" helped to focus national attention on Fiesta. Flambeau had its own queen, except she was called "Miss Fiesta," and she and her float were sent to such diverse events as the Florida Festival of States, the Cherry Blossom Festival in the nation's capital, the Minneapolis Aquatennial, the St. Paul Winter Carnival, and the Tournament of Roses in Pasadena.

From the beginning, the Fiesta Flambeau has been "different." During the more than three decades that Andricks directed it, he liked to add the unexpected. One year one of the many baton twirlers was a shapely fifty-four-year-old grandmother whose claim to fame was that she was a member of the Mothers' Club of Texas A&M University. Allowing her to participate was evidence that Andricks could be ecumenical. As an alumnus of the University of Texas, he felt keen rivalry for the Aggies, and always saw to it that the 350-piece U.T. Longhorn Band led his Flambeau Parade.

Andricks not only included the unusual in the Flambeau, but he would do anything to make sure that nothing stopped the show.

One year he signed Mickey Dolenz, a youngster starring in a TV series called "Elephant Boy," to ride an elephant in the Flambeau. Andricks rented the animal, put the boy and his mother in a downtown hotel, and left them until starting time for the parade. When they failed to arrive on schedule at the assembly point where he awaited them, he hailed a police car and was driven with red lights flashing to the St. Anthony.

The mother and son were having a leisurely meal in the restaurant, but Andricks jerked the boy out of his chair and headed out. It was ten minutes before starting time, and the police car was not immediately visible. Then he saw it parked down the street, but the officer wasn't in it. No matter. Andricks got it started and they headed out Broadway. Later he learned that he had "stolen" a different police car while the driver was inside investigating a robbery. But the parade started on time!

The Flambeau Changes Direction

After Andricks' death in 1984, the Shriners were given the responsibility for Flambeau in 1985. The Jaycees tried their hands as sponsors in 1986.

In addition to the Queens, there is also a Miss Fiesta. In this 1956 photo she receives her crown from Rudolph Richter. Holding her scepter is Reynolds Andricks, who conceived the idea for the Fiesta Flambeau in 1948 and built it into one of the largest night parades staged anywhere.

— San Antonio Express/News *Collection,*
Institute of Texan Cultures

However, the parade somehow lacked the pizazz that had been its trademark for more than three decades, and the Junior Chamber decided to give it up. In 1988 the Fiesta Commission gave it to the League of United Latin American Citizens, Council No. 2 — the same group that elects the Ugly King. When LULAC got into an internal legal wrangle in 1989, a new group known as the Fiesta Flambeau Parade Association took over the event. Their 1990 parade was rated by the press (and the thousands who watched it) as one of the best yet.

The new association is made up of fifty members who pay dues for the privilege and another 150 volunteers. They are dedicated to continuing to make the Flambeau unique. It is not a difficult task. The event is so popular that more than 200 applications are received each year from would-be participants. From these, about 150 are selected. Entries are limited to make sure that the parade won't last too long and will have the variety that has made it a Fiesta favorite.

The goal is to cover the 2.4-mile parade route in about two hours. It always starts promptly at 7:15 P.M., and the sponsors want to end it on schedule so people will not be on the streets too late. In a given year, Flambeau will field some fifty floats, as many as forty bands, up to fourteen groups mounted on horseback, and a collection of clowns, notables, Miss Fiesta, and always some new, special added surprise.

It's flamboyant, fantastic, and exciting. It's Fiesta Flambeau.

11

The Ladies Who Stage
A Night to Eat and Remember

"Women are unpredictable. You never know how they're going to get their own way!"
— **Franklin P. Adams**

They're known in some quarters as the "genteel lady fanatics," the "hysterical sisterhood," and "the little old ladies in tennis shoes," but they are not exclusively female. They include a few men — a very few — among their members. They also have been called feisty, eccentric, and silly. But they like to think of their organization as "the savior of San Antonio," a very apt description of their more than six decades of historic preservation.

They are members of the San Antonio Conservation Society (SACS), chartered on July 11, 1925, a quarter century before the National Trust for Historic Preservation. Since then, they have spent their time, talents, leadership, and money on the keeping and restoring of the old, while using their considerable power to affect the future as well.

For the Conservation Society, Fiesta is the money machine that has made much of its good works possible. Its four-day "Night in Old San Antonio" annually draws to La Villita more than 100,000 revelers who leave some $250,000 net in the society's coffers. These funds are used to acquire historic structures in danger of demolition (its tax-free foundation presently controls more than $2 million in such properties) and to rehabilitate them over time.

The Past is Only Prologue

The society also looks constantly to the future, making sure that its members sit on city boards concerned with zoning, downtown revitalization, additional beautification of the San Antonio River, flood control, and much more. Members say they're not interested in just *remembering* an historic

building. They prefer to say, "Here it is. We helped to save it."

And save it they have. Beginning with their purchase in the early 1930s of parcels of land around the San Jose Mission, they have been buying, preserving, and restoring properties throughout the city. Somehow the money for these activities has always been found, although it was not until SACS joined forces with Fiesta in 1948 and launched its fabulous "Night in Old San Antonio" that its continuing financial success was assured.

The First Project

The beginning of SACS was almost accidental. The organization grew out of a chance meeting one day of two San Antonio women who were history buffs. One, Rena Maverick Green, was the granddaughter of Sam Maverick, the Texas patriot whose stray cattle caused a new word to be added to the regional vocabulary. The other was Emily Edwards, a lady who loved history and believed in acting to preserve its structures.

In their impromptu meeting, they each expressed concern that the old Market House, a neoclassical structure on Market Street, was about to be demolished. They decided to join forces and see if they could save it. They enlisted some friends in their cause, and on March 22, 1924, thirteen women met to form a tiny civic club to be known as the San Antonio Conservation Society. Two men also attended the first meeting but were not invited to membership. Two other women later joined, and the group had fifteen when it was incorporated and chartered the next year.

Emily Edwards, a co-founder and the first president of the San Antonio Conservation Society, photographed at the Spanish Governor's Palace in downtown San Antonio in 1933, eight years after SACS was organized with thirteen charter members.

— San Antonio Light *Collection, Institute of Texan Cultures*

Today membership is just under 3,000. Of these, 650 are active, voting members. Active membership is still hard to come by. Only a few are added annually and only after strong recommendations from those who already enjoy this special status. Associate membership is open to anyone interested in the organization's goals and objectives, and now more than 2,000 of these pay annual dues without having a voice in SACS affairs.

The society is still dominated by women. No man sat on the powerful sixty-three-member board of directors until 1990. Now there are three. For several years, Conrad True held the paid position of administrator, but he was not permitted to attend board meetings. Unlike the women who started Fiesta with their Battle of Flowers, who weren't averse to asking men for financial help, the women of SACS have marched to a different and exclusively female drummer.

Preservation by Piggy Bank

When they have needed help — financial, political, or just encouragement — they have never hesitated to call on men. But their definite, though unwritten, policy of always trying to manage with their own resources dates back more than sixty years. So does their farsighted planning for the preservation of historic landmarks.

On July 5, 1924, a year before the society was chartered, Elizabeth Graham, one of the organizers, advised her colleagues to begin buying property around the city's old missions. She argued that this could be "the first step in protecting" these historic buildings. She believed that one day all of the missions could be brought under the aegis of either the state or national governments and properly restored for posterity.

Since neither of these agencies had expressed interest in the project, the ladies went to work. They staged an open-air Mexican market, four rummage sales, a Mexican dinner, and other activities. At a later meeting, each member was handed a clay piggy bank from Mexico and told to take it home and fill it with pennies.

When the banks were full, the society held a barbecue, broke out the coins, and added them to the fund for the mission lands. This inspired some of the members to make additional cash donations and some others to buy some land parcels themselves and then deed them to SACS. One husband paid $500 for a piece of the land, gave it to his wife as a birthday gift, and she passed it on to the society. When it was discovered that the fund was still short, members borrowed $2,000 to complete the deal.

Making Bail for Property

By 1930, SACS owned $4,500 worth of the acreage around the missions, but they wanted more. Especially desired was the old granary that served San Jose. It had been used as a residence and was in deplorable condition, but it was rehabitable. The problem was that the owner wanted $10,000 — a price the women thought was inflated.

The owner was Ignacio Salcedo, a descendant of the Spanish architect who is believed by some to be the architect and sculptor who built the old mission. In addition to collecting rental from apartments he had created in the granary, he also sold moonshine whiskey as a sideline. This turned out to be a fortuitous circumstance for the SACS ladies when he was arrested on a bootlegging charge and needed $2,000 for bail. He suddenly agreed to cut his asking price for the building in half if he could have $2,500 in immediate cash.

The society's treasury was almost nonexistent, so they went calling again on their friendly banker. However, his friendship was apparently not as strong as they hoped it might be. The minutes of their next SACS meeting reported that the lender explained "gently and politely [that] husbands had to sign the note with their wives." No problem. Not only did each spouse's signature appear, but so did those of both the president and board chairman of the bank. Their collateral: a pile of rocks badly in need of rebuilding.

Title to the property was only the beginning. By begging and borrowing, they went on to restore the granary with the help of WPA laborers. When rehabilitation was complete, it was declared a National Historic Site — the first building outside of the eastern U.S. to win such a designation.

The restoration of the granary was the first step on the long road which Mrs. Graham envisioned for the four missions. Her daughter, Wanda Ford (widow of the late, great San Antonio conservation architect O'Neil Ford), says her mother's vision was to see the four missions joined one day in a national historic park. The dream came true in 1978 when President Jimmy Carter signed legislation appropriating $9.5 million for the first ten-year plan. This provided the first outside assistance for the preservation and restoration of the properties.

It had taken fifty-four years to accomplish, but one of the first projects of the Conservation Society had become a reality.

Other Projects Didn't Wait

These early efforts were only the beginning of an almost unbelieveable transformation of historic San Antonio by the society. The Spanish Governor's Palace, Travis and San Pedro parks, the King William Historic District, and dozens of other buildings and sites important to the city's past have been saved from destruction and rehabilitated through the efforts of SACS. Members admit, however, that San Pedro Park still needs a lot of "saving."

As might be expected, not all of its projects have had the unstinted support of the citizens. As related in an earlier chapter, the successful effort of SACS to save the San Antonio River from being paved over to become a parking lot met strong opposition from the very merchants who would benefit most when it became a tourist attraction. Years after the north expressway finally was built through part of Brackenridge Park and Olmos Basin, there are still those who refuse to support SACS because it forced a ten-year delay of the project.

By any standard, the San Antonio Conservation Society today is one of the largest, strongest, and richest organizations of its kind in America. Its work has had an impact far outside the city it was formed to serve. In 1975 it lobbied an ordinance setting up an historic preservation office to review all demolition requests and for planned construction in historic areas. It also managed to get a SACS board member, Pat Osborne, appointed to administer the job. The action opened the door for other cities to follow suit and many have.

It also led the way for the nation in getting whole neighborhoods and even business sections of a city declared historic districts with all future changes in these areas strictly regulated by tough zoning laws. The King William area became the

Rena Maverick Green, one of the co-founders in 1924 of the San Antonio Conservation Society. She was the granddaughter of Sam Maverick, the Texas patriot whose stray cattle caused a new word, "maverick," to be added to the vocabulary.

— *San Antonio Conservation Society*

first in 1968. Since then, six other parts of the city have been so designated and the society continues to push for others.

Much of SACS' success has been because of the political clout that it has built over the years and the size of its bankroll. For the latter, it is forever indebted to Fiesta San Antonio and the opportunity to present those four magical evenings in La Villita known as "A Night in Old San Antonio."

The hundreds of thousands who have been a part of these "nights" over the years have another name for the event: "A night to eat and remember." The next chapter tells why.

Above: Gen. Douglas MacArthur, who attended Texas Military Institute while his father commanded Fort Sam Houston, returned to San Antonio in 1953 to join the Daughters of the Republic of Texas pilgrimage to the Alamo at Fiesta.

— *Joe Elicson Collection, Institute of Texan Cultures*

Left: The late Mayor Maury Maverick, who helped members of the San Antonio Conservation Society in their efforts to beautify the river, is shown here making the opening speech at the first River Parade in 1936.

— San Antonio Light *Collection, Institute of Texan Cultures*

*Above:*For a decade, one of the highlights of the celebration was La Noche de Fiesta, sponsored by the Mexican American Chamber of Commerce. In 1940, Atlee B. Ayres designed this elaborate stage setting which represented a plaza in Taxco, Mexico.

— *Ann Russell Collection, Institute of Texan Cultures*

Right: After the Indians and Spaniards, Germans were among San Antonio's earliest settlers. They still form a large segment of the population. Here Lester Noble represents Hermann, the Cherusker, at Hermann's Happiness, a Fiesta event since 1979.

— *Fiesta San Antonio Commission*

Above: San Antonio's League of United Latin American Citizens elected its first El Rey Feo (The Ugly King) in 1947 as a device to raise scholarship funds for deserving Hispanics. It was not until 1979, however, when Logan Stewart assumed the throne, that the Ugly King achieved royal status in the Fiesta hierarchy. He is shown with two aides as he began a tour of schools, hospitals, and nursing homes during the 1980 Fiesta San Antonio.

— *Fiesta San Antonio Commission*

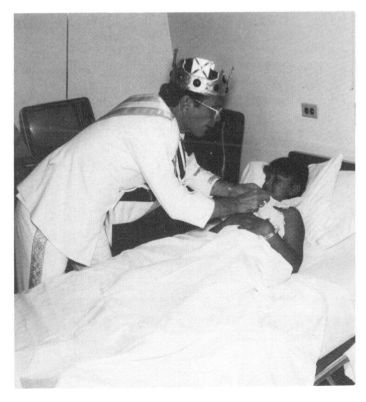

Left: In the more than forty years that there has been an El Rey Feo, many Anglos have been given the honor. Here Ugly King Dennis O'Malley comforts a young patient on one of his hospital visits.

— *Photo courtesy of Marco Mendiola*

Above: The Cornyation pokes fun at the elaborate Coronation of the Order of the Alamo's Queen. For twenty-five years, this bit of satirical naughtiness has played a unique and interesting role in Fiesta.

— San Antonio Express/News
Collection, Institute of Texan Cultures

Below: El Rey Feo disdains a horse-drawn carriage in favor of an elaborate float. Here Larry Raba, the 1988 Ugly King, waves to crowds as the parade passes the Menger Hotel.

— *Fiesta San Antonio Commission*

Fiesta San Antonio attracts visitors from throughout the country and many foreign countries. Here the Continental Color Guard and the Fife and Drum Corps, both elements of the 3rd U.S. Infantry at Fort Myers, Virginia, participate in the Fiesta Quadrangle Ceremony at San Antonio's Fort Sam Houston.

— TASC Photo Facility, Fort Sam Houston

Lots of military bands appear in Fiesta parades, but not all march. In the Battle of Flowers Parade of 1957, the Fort Hood U.S. Army Band rode in Jeeps.

— Zintgraff Collection, Institute of Texan Cultures

Above: For sixty years, a Children's Fete was a part of Fiesta. This group, dressed as butterflies, was photographed in the 1920s. Today dozens of Fiesta events still involve children of all ages.

— Lewison Studio

Below: Children dominated the floats in early Battle of Flowers parades. Fiesta was less than a decade old when this photograph was made.

— San Antonio Museum Association

A portrait of Mrs. H. D. Kampmann, circa 1890, about the time she was named the first chairman of the Battle of Flowers Association.

— *Courtesy of Ike D. Kampmann*

At the Fiesta Oyster Bake on the campus of St. Mary's University, about 50,000 slurp down as many as 100,000 of this gourmet seafood. Like most Fiesta events, the Oyster Bake features continuous music.

— *Al Rendon*

The Arts Fair, staged on the Southwest Crafts Center's sprawling five-acre riverside campus, is one of Fiesta's most family-oriented events. In addition to art, it features the most exotic foods of any Fiesta event, includes a Children's Art Contest, and offers children and adults a chance to practice arts and crafts in the Experience Courtyard.

— *Al Rendon*

El Mercado, or Market Square, is as old as the first Spanish settlement in San Antonio. The Market Square stages its own mini Fiesta a few blocks west of the river, with food and music featuring the top Tejano and *conjunto* stars, plus country/western, rock, and jazz performers.

— *Al Rendon*

Subjects of the legendary El Rey Feo (The Ugly King) present him with a live goat as a gesture of ridicule for the real King. San Antonio's El Rey Feo Carlos Madrid receives the traditional goat from Marco Mendiola.

— *Photo courtesy of Marco Mendiola*

Today as many as 500,000 people gather to watch the Battle of Flowers, the only parade in the U.S. planned and staged entirely by women.

— *Al Rendon*

"A night to remember" is the way Fiesta-goers describe A Night in Old San Antonio, the largest non-parade event in the celebration.

— *San Antonio Conservation Society*

The San Antonio Conservation Society, which boasts some 650 voting members and more than 2,000 associates, headquarters in the beautiful Wulff House in the city's historic King William District.

— *Al Rendon*

Residents of the King William District near downtown began staging a neighborhood fair in 1968. It's another Fiesta family favorite. The first National Historic District in all of Texas opens some homes to tours and provides blocks of food booths and a variety of entertainment for all ages. The Steves Home, shown here, and the old Arsenal are in the district.

— *Al Rendon*

A Mexican *charreada*, or rodeo, is one of the unique events of Fiesta San Antonio. The *charreada* originated in the 1550s with Mexican *rancheros* who wanted to show off the horsemanship of their *charros*. It became the model for American rodeos, which originated in Texas.

— *Al Rendon*

The annual Fiesta Run from the Alamo to San Jose Mission attracts hundreds of participants and raises money for charities.

— *Al Rendon*

Children have a role in dozens of Fiesta events. This special party for *los niños*, sponsored by the Jaycees, precedes the opening of their La Semana Alegre.

— *Al Rendon*

The dozens of food booths and beverage centers guarantee that NIOSA is the place to eat, drink, and be merry.

— Al Rendon

The Queen chosen by the Order of the Alamo is not the only royalty visible at Fiesta. Here the Charro's Queen congratulates a finalist in the competition for her crown.

— Al Rendon

Over a century, the Coronation has grown into a spectacle that rivals a Broadway production and plays to a full house of San Antonio's elite. This was the way La Corte de la Tierra Magica received guests in 1975.
— *Zintgraff Collection, Institute of Texan Cultures*

Responsibility for planning and staging the 100th anniversary of Fiesta in 1991 rests with these members of the commission's executive committee and the centennial coordinator. They are (top row, left to right): Thad Ziegler, president, Texas Cavaliers; Paul Rossbach, presidential appointee; Rick Noll, president, Fiesta Flambeau Association; Jack Saunders, secretary, Fiesta Commission; Dr. William Thornton, Fiesta Commission vice-president; and Pete Martinez, treasurer. (Middle row): Maurice Toppin, president, Alamo Square and Round Dance Club; Frank Sammis, president, Order of the Alamo; Donald Moye, vice-president, and Bob Carlson, senior vice-president, Fiesta San Antonio Commission. (Front row): Marleen Pedroza, executive vice-president, Fiesta Commission; Inell Schooler, immediate past president of the commission; Barbara Wenger, 1991 president; Jane Foster, president, San Antonio Conservation Society; Elaine Persyne, president, St. Luke's Festival Association; and Joanna Parrish, coordinator of the Centennial Festival. Not pictured is Morgia Lepick, president of the Battle of Flowers Association.

— *Al Rendon*

San Antonio's many ethnic groups plan special events as a part of their celebration of Fiesta. Here costumed singers perform at the Garden Festival at Beethoven Hall.

— *Allensworth*

The University of Texas Longhorn Band marches past the Alamo while crowds in the stands cheer.

— *Al Rendon*

Bands make any parade, and dozens of them participate in those staged at Fiesta.

— Al Rendon

The famed Marching Band of Texas A&M University has been a part of Fiesta for many years.

Fiesta Flambeau was led by the University of Texas Longhorn Band during the years that Reynolds Andricks had charge of this lighted extravaganza. Andricks, a UT alumnus, insisted that his alma mater's band receive this honor.

— *Fiesta San Antonio Commission*

Since 1935, the Battle of Flowers Association's Band Festival has been filling Alamo Stadium with spectators to watch up to thirty selected high school brass ensembles perform.

— *Charles J. Long*

The Texas Cavaliers' float in the River Parade always brings cheers from the thousands of spectators.

— *Al Rendon*

San Antonio no longer is a frontier city, but Fiesta parade floats like this one remind the city of its beginnings more than 350 years ago.

— *Al Rendon*

Although their blooms today are mostly artificial, every float in the Battle of Flowers Parade carries out the original theme.

— *Gary Perkins*

Fiesta parade floats aren't all flowers. This one represents one of Texas' favorite crops, the watermelon.

— Al Rendon

The good ship *Lollipop*, lighted from bow to stern, sails in the Fiesta Flambeau.

— Al Rendon

Fiesta extends throughout the city. In addition to events like the San Antonio Jaycees' La Semana Alegre downtown, the Cactus and Xerophyte Show at Central Park Mall, and dozens of others, strolling bands, dancers, and singers visit offices and residences about town. Lois Marie Coulon, age thirteen, dances in this 1939 photo with Will Rogers and his musicians.

San Antonio Light *Collection, Institute of Texan Cultures*

Above: Fiesta parade floats over the years have ranged from the elaborate to the ridiculous to the homemade. This 1951 entry of the Paricutin Club is a good example of the latter. It was designed and constructed entirely by club members. Bebe Canales Inkley is the young woman waving to the crowd.

— *Fiesta San Antonio Commission*

Left: The annual pilgrimage to the Alamo, sponsored by the Daughters of the Republic of Texas, is one of the most moving events of Fiesta. Several hundred people representing schools, as well as historical, civic, military and other groups, march in solemn procession from the Municipal Auditorium and place wreaths at the cradle of Texas liberty to honor the 189 who died there in 1836.

— San Antonio Express/News
Collection, Institute of Texan Cultures

Baking enough oysters to serve 50,000 people keeps the volunteers of St. Mary's University alumni association busy preparing for one of Fiesta's most popular events.
— *St. Mary's University*

What would Fiesta be without a Taste of New Orleans? Staged at the Sunken Gardens in Brackenridge Park, this event attracts thousands who love jazz, good food, and fellowship.

— *Fiesta San Antonio Commission*

Left: Tripping the light fantastic is a Fiesta tradition. Everywhere there are folk, ethnic, and square dances, plus formal balls. The ball shown here has been staged by the Pioneer Association since 1918.

— *Zintgraff Collection, Institute of Texan Cultures*

Main Plaza, photographed in the early 1900s, always has been a place of gaiety and fiesta in San Antonio. When Lieutenant Zebulon Pike's expedition visited the Villa de Bejar in 1807, he wrote that acrobats, clowns, and tumblers entertained on the plazas and in the streets.

— *San Antonio Conservation Society photo*

A popular Fiesta event in past years was the Trades Day Parade, when local businesses showed off their wares. In 1930, Joske's, for years the city's leading department store, used this float to demonstrate advances in home laundering.

— Lewison Studio

Above: Gondolas — at least, the American version — are not strangers to the river. This one, sponsored by the San Antonio Conservation Society, was an entry in the Texas Cavaliers' River Parade in the 1960s.

— *Joe Elicson Collection, Daughters of the Republic of Texas Library*

Left: The Flower Show, sponsored by the Woman's Club, is one of the oldest Fiesta events. In this 1929 photo, Mrs. Beaumont B. Buck poses with an arrangement. Held for years at the Gunter Hotel, the show is now staged at a shopping mall.

— San Antonio Light *Collection, Institute of Texan Cultures*

 **12**

Eat, Drink, and Be Merry

"It is the part of a wise man to feed himself with moderate food and drink, and to take pleasure with . . . dress, music, sports, and theatres and other places of this kind . . ."

— **Spinoza** (1632–1677)

San Antonio has mastered the art of making visitors feel uncommonly welcome. One of the ways in which it demonstrates this is during the twenty frenzied hours over four days when up to 100,000 people crowd into La Villita for what is the biggest — and many consider the best — single event of Fiesta.

It's called "A Night in Old San Antonio," and that's exactly what it was when it began on April 21, 1948. That first NIOSA, at which the only foods served were barbecue, beans, and coffee for a net profit of $2,586, has expanded into four succeeding "nights" when 16,000 volunteers serve a cornucopia of exotic ethnic dishes, music, and dance to the revelers. The event adds more than $250,000 annually to the coffers of the sponsoring San Antonio Conservation Society.

Food, drink, and a variety of entertainment were hard to come by at the first Battle of Flowers in 1891. Those who were hungry after the parade either sampled the wares of the Mexican chili queens around Main Plaza, went home to dinner, or dropped in at the Menger Hotel Colonial Room across from the Alamo and had a seven-course meal for $1.50. In either place, the meal likely would include dishes of German or Mexican origin, with perhaps a purely Texan dessert like pecan pie.

Not so at Fiesta today, as a recent visitor demonstrated. He took one look at some of the menus offered at dozens of different events, including NIOSA, and vowed to start on opening day to eat all of his meals on site until the annual festival closed. His only stipulation was that each menu had to feature at least one entrée with which he was not familiar. In ten days, he tried thirty bills of fare at as many food booths. He was pleased with his ac-

complishment until he discovered later that he missed at least 150 more, almost all offering dishes he had never tried.

Take Your Choice from 300 Viands

The amount and variety of food consumed at a single Fiesta is incredible. The one-day Oyster Bake at St. Mary's University requires 90,000 of the bivalves, not to mention the fried catfish, eggrolls, crepes, and onion rings. At Hermann's Happiness, there is Kuh Schtik and a variety of other German delicacies. The Israeli Festival features kosher dishes comparable to those available in the best hotels in Jerusalem. And so on through a lengthy cookbook of other comestibles designed to please virtually every ethnic taste imaginable.

It is estimated that there are more than 300 foods available at a given Fiesta. They represent the best recipes of the thirty-plus ethnic and cultural groups that settled and developed San Antonio and who are still coming from around the world to live there. The greatest variety is available only at NIOSA because it operates fifteen food areas, each devoted to a variety of ethnic specialties. The menus change each year because NIOSA planners now use computers to determine the dishes that have proved to be the most palate-pleasing.

Barbacoa, the barbecued head of a calf, although a popular Mexican dish, is no longer available at NIOSA because it is served at so many restaurants. *Menudo*, a dish made from tripe (the lining of a cow's stomach), also has disappeared from the NIOSA menu. But *anticuchos*, spicy, charcoal-broiled chunks of beef marinated in spices, remain a perennial best-seller. NIOSA inspired the blending

After its beginnings in 1937 at San Jose Mission, the forerunner of A Night in Old San Antonio was moved downtown to the river. It was renamed the River Festival, then the River Jubilee. In 1948 it became an official part of Fiesta and became A Night in Old San Antonio.

— *San Antonio Conservation Society*

Above: Not all Battle of Flowers Parade floats have been lavishly decorated with beautiful flora. In the 1947 parade, a local dude ranch used only hay and pretty girls as its entry.

— San Antonio Light *Collection, Institute of Texan Cultures*

Left: Ethel Wilson Harris was the "mother" of NIOSA. In 1937, she was resident curator at San Jose Mission and conceived an Indian Festival on the grounds as a fund-raiser for SACS. Elizabeth Graham, a charter member of SACS, was the first chairman. This event later was moved downtown and called the River Jubilee and later River Festival. On April 21, 1948, it was moved to historic La Villita, renamed Night in Old San Antonio, and has been a major Fiesta event since.

— San Antonio Conservation Society

of a Polish sausage and a Mexican tortilla into a delight called a Taco Polaco.

Whatever Fiesta specialty diners may choose, they want it served as finger food and not as a full plate. They like to try small amounts of a variety of things. Even the turkey legs are from hens rather than toms because they're smaller and less filling. About the only standard-size offering served is the hamburger.

This delicacy, of course, is pure Texan. It was invented in an East Texas drug store soda fountain about the same time the first Battle of Flowers was being staged on Alamo Plaza. A short-order cook named Fletcher Davis of Athens made a sandwich of ground beef one day as an experiment. It became so popular that the local Chamber of Commerce sent him to the 1904 St. Louis World's Fair to serve it there. It proved to be such a culinary coup that the *New York Herald-Tribune* published a feature about it. Despite the claims of Hamburg, Germany, and others, even researchers at McDonald's, the world's largest purveyor of the hamburger, agree that it originated in Texas.

More Than Just Food

Entertainment as well as food has been emphasized since NIOSA had its beginnings in 1937 as a small Indian Festival at San Jose Mission. Ethel Harris, an early president of the San Antonio Conservation Society, was the mission curator and saw a small festival as a way both to raise needed funds for SACS and to focus public attention on its efforts at historic preservation. Later the event was moved downtown and called the River Festival and then the River Jubilee. It was not a part of Fiesta but was held annually in the bend of the San Antonio River near the old Travis Hotel.

The area was divided into ten sections: Indian, Spanish, Mexican, Texan, Pioneer, Old South, Western, Gay Nineties, Artists, and Carnival. Each section had a chairman and a boat. Festivities began with a band of Indians leading the boats downstream to their designated docks. Riding the boats were San Antonio's leading citizens, wearing costumes of the Gay Nineties or of their ethnic heritage.

Floating food service was available, as some boats sold bean tacos for a dime each to passengers floating by on other rafts. Once the boats docked, a program was presented on the river theater stage. The evening then continued with food and dancing in Navarro Plaza (now the La Villita Assembly Building). These events raised some funds for SACS, but were supplemented with other efforts such as dinners at the Spanish Governor's Palace, whose restoration it had pushed.

The River Jubilee Joins Fiesta

By 1948, the River Jubilee had grown into such a popular event that SACS was invited to include it in Fiesta. It was given a new name: A Night in Old San Antonio. And its new site was La Villita, the historic village on the river in the heart of downtown. Villita Street was roped off at either end and along its length were bazaars, vendors, and the stands of the old-time chili queens. The members of SACS, attempting to create an Old World atmosphere, were costumed to represent each phase of the city's existence. This was emphasized by goats and geese which wandered around and tried to avoid the feet of the visitors and dancers.

The first NIOSA was a combination arts and craft show/food fair and festival. The art galleries, artists' studios, and crafts shops that still populate La Villita were open, traditional chuck wagons served full-course barbecue dinners, and there were exhibitions of Mexican and Spanish folk dancing. Those preferring less food lined up at the charcoal stoves of the chili queens.

Food for the Gods

Chili was, is, and probably ever shall be a favorite NIOSA food, although Maria's famed tortillas and *anticuchos* give it a run in popularity. Like the hamburger, chili is another delicacy that is pure Texas. Even Mexico concedes this.

The *Dictionario de Mejicanismos* says this: "Chili con carne: detestable food passing itself off as Mexican, sold in the U.S. from Texas to New York."

Texans have never considered their national dish, chili, as detestable. Maury Maverick, Jr., son of the mayor who was among those who led the effort to beautify the river, once described the "bowl of red" as "God's special San Antonio blessing." Thus those who enjoy chili at A Night in Old San Antonio should know that at least one historian says it originated on the spot where they're standing.

She is Ella K. Daggett Stumpf, a member of SACS for more than half a century and the resident authority on local culinary subjects. Writing in the March 1978 issue of *San Antonio Magazine*, she thoroughly documents the fact that the first *chile con carne* undoubtedly resulted from the effort of a Payaya Indian squaw cutting beef jerky into strips and boiling them on a fire outside their La Villita *jacal*.

The result was far removed from the succulent dish now served at NIOSA. The first improvement to the recipe came when the Spanish soldiers and the Catholic *padres* arrived, followed by the Canary Islanders in 1731. They brought with them cumin seeds, now a necessary ingredient of first-rate chili. Later wild onions were added, along with garlic and the inevitable peppers. Thus the first *chile con carne*, San Antonio-style, had arrived, and it would take the nation by storm.

It was San Antonians, however, who were first to succumb to what one aficionado has described as "food for the gods." The late humorist H. Allen Smith, who liked the dish so well that he left New York to live out his life in the Big Bend, once said: "Chili in Texas is a religion." It's also a law. A few years back, the legislature passed a resolution making chili the state's official dish.

At least six decades before the first NIOSA, the so-called "chili queens" had made San Antonio a unique tourist attraction. These women would appear each evening on the downtown plaza with carts loaded with pots of chili. As the stars came out, they would set up tables and chairs and lamps to attract customers. Then they would light mesquite wood fires under their earthen pots and wait for the aroma to signal that food was ready. Guests at the Menger and other nearby hotels would walk to the plazas for an unusual culinary experience. It was not until late in this century that the chili queens were forever banned by health authorities as "unsanitary."

Even Chili Powder and Fritos Started Here

That these open-air kitchens didn't pass muster with the local bureaucrats never bothered the customers. They ate the succulent stew and enjoyed it, but grumbled because they couldn't reproduce it at home. One of those was William Gebhardt, a visitor from New Braunfels. He decided to try to invent a powder that would supply the needed ingredients for home chefs. He ground ancho peppers — the broad red ones used in the best chili — and combined them with oregano, cumin seeds, and garlic. Soon Gebhardt's Chili Powder (manufactured in San Antonio) became as common an item in pantries as K.C. Baking Powder and P&G Soap.

Along with chili at NIOSA are other Mexican (more accurately Tex-Mex) foods ranging from burritos (soft tacos filled with ground meat, cheese, etc.) to *buñuelos* (a taco fried thin and sprinkled with sugar and cinnamon). Most will be served, even if one orders a hamburger, with another San Antonio invention, the corn chip.

They are best known by their predominant trade name, Fritos, and Americans annually eat 200 million pounds of them at NIOSA and elsewhere. They are the creation of a Mexican whose name is lost to history but who had a small restaurant in San Antonio in 1932. One day Elmer Doolin stopped in for a nickel sandwich, paid another nickel for a package of homemade corn chips, and thus started on his way to change the habits of snack-loving Americans.

He liked the taste of the chip, and when the Mexican decided to sell his restaurant, Doolin bought the recipe for $100. He produced his first batch in his mother's kitchen on Roosevelt Avenue, named them Fritos, and started selling them from his Model-T Ford. Cooking the chips at night, he constantly worked to achieve the right combination of corn for the *masa*. He also developed a system to form the chips exactly an inch and a half long, half an inch wide, and 70/100ths of an inch thick. He peddled them by day, grossing between $8 and $10 per batch. In 1933 he moved to Dallas, started the Frito Company, and soon dominated the snack food market. When he died, the company was merged with a potato chip manufacturer, but his product is still widely distributed.

From Calf Fries to Beignets

At NIOSA, Fritos are a condiment for many items that are not Mexican. They often replace French fries served with a dish known as "calf fries" — the testicles of a steer. On the other hand, Norse Dilstix, a fried dill pickle served by the Norwegians, is served straight. The French Quarter's "beignets" require no accompaniment except coffee.

Since Germans comprise the state's fourth largest ethnic group, their Biergarten is one of NIOSA's favorite watering places. It also offers a line of favorite foods from the Fatherland. In recent years, an addition to the ever-changing menu has been "soul food."

For the uninitiated, "soul food" is not a definitive term describing a particular comestible or cooking style. According to the researchers at San Antonio's University of Texas Institute of Texan Cultures, it is any food meant to convey a feeling of kinship. It has been been prepared for years by

There's something for everybody at NIOSA. The Bird in the Gilded Cage brought along her own body-guards in a 1960s celebration.

— *Zintgraff Collection, Institute of Texan Cultures*

both whites and blacks.

It is its link to slavery, however, that distinguishes modern soul food from other types of Southern cuisine. Slaves often were given only those parts of the hog that the master didn't want, such as the ears, feet, and internal organs. These throwaways were taken by the slaves and made into dishes like hog maw or chitterlings ("chittlins," in the vernacular). Supplemented by black-eyed peas and salad made of wild poke greens, along with an occasional squirrel, rabbit or possum, these made up the staple diet of slaves before Emancipation.

After they were given their freeedom, most blacks still couldn't afford expensive cuts of meat. Thus throwaways like pig ears, intestines, and other parts of the animal continued to be important to the family menu and are the soul foods of today. Prepared correctly, they are a delicacy.

More Than A One-Night Stand

Food, plus good entertainment, has been the secret of the growth of NIOSA from a one-night stand to four days of fun, flair, and frolic. In the early years, two members of SACS, Ethel Harris and Elizabeth Graham, owned all of the tables, chairs, and equipment used in producing NIOSA and decorated all of the booths themselves. When it was suggested in 1954 that they add a second night to the event, the members, horrified at the additional work that would be required, voted a resounding "no."

This didn't stop Mrs. Harris, who had suggested the idea. She contacted the wives' clubs at the military installations and offered to designate the addition as Armed Forces Night. All went well until most of their military husbands were suddenly transferred to other posts shortly before Fiesta and the SACS ladies were faced with doing it all them-

Elizabeth Graham, a founder of the Conservation Society, along with Ethel Harris, conceived the idea of a River Jubilee as a fund-raiser. It began as a one-night affair in 1937 and was the predecessor of A Night in Old San Antonio. NIOSA was staged for the first time in 1948, also as a one-night event. Today it runs for four nights.

— *San Antonio Conservation Society*

selves. They rallied, had one of their most successful NIOSAs, and decided to add a third night three years later in 1957. In 1958 they added the fourth night — a plan that isn't likely to be changed.

The ranching tradition still runs deep in Texas and cowgirls (and cowboys) mingle with the royalty at Fiesta.

— *Lewison Studio, San Antonio Museum Association Collection*

An old-fashioned street carnival has been a Fiesta event for decades. At one time, the tents and rides were erected along the main route of the Battle of Flowers Parade. In this 1910 scene, a military contingent leads a decorated carriage past a carnival sideshow tent.

— *San Antonio Museum Association Collection*

13

The Many Faces of Fiesta

"It is the common wonder of all men how among so many millions of faces there should be none alike."

— **Sir Thomas Browne,** 1642

Fiesta San Antonio is deeply rooted in the military. So is the city.

Almost from its beginnings, San Antonio has been a fortress. "Discovered" by the Spanish in 1691, the Spanish governor founded a garrison at San Antonio de Bejar in 1718 because it was halfway between the Catholic missions in East Texas and the presidio of northern Mexico in Saltillo. In the 300 years since, all sorts of warfare has been staged in and around San Antonio. The annihilation of the Alamo defenders on March 6, 1836, remains one of the most famous battles in world history.

Fiesta itself began with a "battle." The parade of carriages around Alamo Plaza that April day in 1891 was like a planned military engagement. It was staged for one purpose: to honor the heroes who, fifty-five years before, had won Texas its independence from Mexico on the San Jacinto plain. That the ladies in the carriages used flowers rather than bullets to pelt each other was deliberately symbolic of Sam Houston's defeat of Santa Anna. They even named the occasion the "Battle of Flowers," and that name has remained for a century.

From the beginning of Fiesta, the military has had an active role. Fort Sam Houston had been established in 1879, and two army officers stationed there helped in the planning of the first Battle of Flowers. Fort Sam, now headquarters for the 5th Army and one of the nation's oldest military posts still in use, has been a part of the celebration since.

The role of the military has grown as more installations were built. In addition to Fort Sam Houston, four air bases — Brooks, Kelly, Lackland, and Randolph — surround the city. Brooke Army Medical Center and Wilford Hall Air Force Hospi-

tal comprise the world's largest military medical facility. Every Air Force recruit goes through Lackland for basic training. Kelly Field's Air Logistics Center is San Antonio's largest single employer, requiring thousands of civilian experts to repair, overhaul, and modify the nation's Air Force planes.

In fact, the Air Force was born in San Antonio, an event which military floats in Fiesta parades have memorialized occasionally. Historic Fort Sam Houston was the site. There on March 10, 1910, a young Signal Corps first lieutenant, Benjamin D. Foulois, lifted a Wright Type "A" biplane off the parade ground dirt to send a U.S. war machine into the wild blue yonder. It was the first military flight by an American and launched what was originally known as the Army Air Corps.

An Integral Part of Fiesta

At last count, some 350 active or retired generals have called San Antonio home, and most have been actively involved in Fiesta at one time or another. A complete list of such participants is too long to give here, but it would include a youngster named Douglas MacArthur, who marched in a couple of Fiesta parades while he was a Texas Military Institute cadet and his father, Gen. Arthur MacArthur, was commanding Fort Sam.

At the April 21, 1917, luncheon of the Battle of Flowers Association, Gen. John J. Pershing was the speaker shortly before his departure to take command of the American Expeditionary Forces in World War I. His home, Pershing House, is still the official residence at Fort Sam of the commanding general of the 5th Army. Charles A. Lindbergh is but one of the famous names in aviation history

Ellis Shapiro (right), a New York public relations man who adopted San Antonio as his home, became the first executive vice-president of the Fiesta San Antonio Commission. He is shown here presenting a Band Festival Award to John Pearson of MacArthur High School.

— *Harichrome Studio*

page 17 / photo 130

who knew Fiesta while he was winning his wings at Brooks and Kelly Fields.

Today military involvement in Fiesta has been formalized. Each year, a senior officer (commanding general) of one of the Army or Air Force bases is named coordinator. He then asks the commanders of the various installations to name project officers for their commands. These work closely with the Fiesta San Antonio Commission in arranging all aspects of the military-civilian effort.

A written agreement between the military and the commission spells out what equipment and other assistance is to be furnished. The Fiesta Commission also executes a "hold harmless" document protecting the government from liabilities, losses, or damages that may result, and it purchases the necessary liability insurance.

Thus has the military become an integral part of Fiesta. This includes importing bands and marching units from distant installations as well as utilizing the local groups. Air Force bases open for visitors and present special shows and reviews. So does Fort Sam Houston. The various units elect Queens and Ambassadors to participate in Fiesta.

The Music Goes 'Round and 'Round

However, when it comes to music, the military participation is dwarfed by civilian groups.

Since 1935, the Battle of Flowers Association's Annual Band Festival has been packing up to thirty selected high school brass ensembles into Alamo Stadium for one evening. The Battle of Flowers, Flambeau, and the floating parade of the Texas Cavaliers feature virtually every kind of music that can be tooted, plucked, picked, or strummed.

Rock, hard and soft, is featured at La Semana Alegre, the Junior Chamber of Commerce's contribution to Fiesta in HemisFair Park. Blues fanciers congregate at the Institute of Texan Cultures for a free concert featuring the best bluesmen in the state.

There is even a calliope making Fiesta music. One is at the street carnival staged around City Hall. At Fiesta, the streets around that temple of government become clogged with ferris wheels, kiddie rides, booths offering prizes in games of chance, variety shows and the like. This is a real carnival, completely unlike the one that often goes on in the Council Chamber of the imposing building that is the city's headquarters. Another calliope is in Clown Alley in the children's area at A Night in Old San Antonio. Mayor Lila Cockrell was a frequent

performer on both instruments. The Mexican Market, a short distance away, doesn't have one of the steam-powered, organlike monsters that emit notes as ear-shattering whistles. But the Market, renamed the Fiesta del Mercado for the occasion, offers *mariachis*, *cerveza*, festive foods, conversation, and fascinating shopping.

Once limited to downtown and centered around Alamo Plaza, Fiesta today is dispersed throughout the city and likely will continue to spread. During Fiesta Week, there are special events at the large shopping malls off the interstates and even on college campuses. One of the largest single celebrations is the Oyster Bake at St. Mary's University. Another is the Fiesta UTSA at the University of Texas at San Antonio. The University of Texas Health Science Center draws thousands for its Fiesta de Tejas. Our Lady of the Lake University sponsors a Fiesta Spring Jam.

La Villita is Not the Only Fiesta Historic Site

To date, at least, no leprechauns have been sighted at Shenanigan's O'Fair at Incarnate Word College, but well they may be some year. That's because the fair actually is staged on the site of Avoca, an early Irish settlement. Built for 200 families at the headwaters of the San Antonio River shortly after the fall of the Alamo in 1836, it was named after a spot in County Wicklow, Ireland. Another settlement near downtown was known as the Irish Flats.

A favorite family event is the one-day King William Fair, staged since 1978 in the first area in Texas to be declared a National Historic District. The fair begins with its own parade (one of at least a dozen big and little ones around the city during the celebration) and opens its beautifully restored old homes for touring.

The *Charros* Do It Best

One unique presentation is rarely seen outside of Mexico except at Fiesta San Antonio: a Mexican *charreada*, or rodeo. The highlight of two celebrations known as Day in Old Mexico, it is staged at the beginning and end of Fiesta in an arena owned by the Federation of Charros.

The *charreada* was originated in the 1550s by wealthy Mexican *rancheros* who wanted to show off their horsemanship. It became the model for rodeo as Americans know it today. Incidentally, rodeo as a U.S. sport originated in Texas and is only eight years older than the Battle of Flowers. On July 4, 1883, cowboys from several ranches surrounding Pecos, in West Texas, gathered on a vacant lot in that town to demonstrate which outfit was best at riding and roping. It was the first such event in the U.S. where cash prizes were awarded the winners. Pecos' claim is supported by such authorities as the *Encyclopedia Britannica* and others.

Rodeo, except for the *charreada,* has never been a part of Fiesta, possibly because the Anglo version is mild compared to the one from south of the border. The three-hour *charreada* has nine events, with the major feature being one called *colas,* or tails. Three teams of six *charros* each compete. A steer is loosed from the corral and each mounted rider chases it down a runway, salutes it, and then reaches down and tries to grab the animal's tail.

If he succeeds, he has a specified time in which to wrap the tail around his ankle and bring the steer to its knees. The winner is the *charro* who can accomplish the feat in the shortest time.

It's unfortunate that since there are only 2,000 seats for each of the two performances of the *charreada* (standing room for some 300 more), most Fiesta visitors haven't seen it. The same is true for another humorous and naughty event called the Cornyation.

A Little Corny Fun

Back in 1975, some members of the San Antonio Little Theater thought that it would be in order to poke a little fun at the pretentious Fiesta royalty. They decided to elevate two of their own to thrones in a ceremony called the Cornyation and allow the public to aid their drama group by paying for the privilege of attending. Since this all happens in 640-seat Beethoven Hall on HemisFair Plaza, it is repeated on three successive nights for a standing-room-only crowd, and many more are turned away.

This shortage of seating undoubtedly pleases the Order of the Alamo's Queen and her distinguished Court. It's not that they mind having another competing throne in Fiesta, but they don't always relish the humorous mockery of their Court that accompanies the elevation to royalty of King Anchovy and his Queen. However, the Cornyation doesn't limit its lampooning to the rich and the famous who pay as much as $30 to watch the Coronation in Municipal Auditorium. They also aim their barbs at a variety of political, social, and cultural events around the city. The script may not be as sophisticated as that at Washington's famed

Gridiron Dinner, but its country humor is enjoyed by those lucky enough to get a seat.

A crowd-pleasing attraction of the Cornyation are the titles assigned to the royal personages and their dukes and duchesses as well as the outlandish costuming. One year the Queen of the Not So Grand Canal appeared as a San Antonio River Barge. Her headpiece was a six-foot-long reproduction of a barge, complete with miniature camera-toting tourists. To add more realism, there were stuffed flying grackles, the noisy black birds that harass strollers along the stream.

What Egg-Zactly Are *Cascarones?*

Whether it's at the Cornyation, the *charreada,* or even the impressive staid Coronation of the Queen, there is one symbol of Fiesta that is encountered everywhere: a *cascaron.* It's a pretty but nefarious device made by filling an empty eggshell with confetti. As many as 100,000 of them are used at Fiesta each year to prove to Yankees (and Texans who don't call San Antonio home) that it is more blessed to give than receive. Fiesta-goers pay fifty cents each (three for a dollar at some stands) for the fun of cracking up the event by smashing these missles on the heads of the unwary.

There are two stories about the *cascaron's* origin, one true and the other purely apocryphal. Mike Tolson, a columnist for the *San Antonio Light,* concocted the latter version several years ago and it belongs in the folklore of Texas. Following is a condensed version of his story.

It was invented, he claimed, by the man for whom it is named — Casimir Caron. The owner of a West Side restaurant early in this century, Caron also had very strong political views. Seeking a way to disperse his unpopular ideas anonymously, he wrote them on tiny slips of paper and had his chef insert them into empty eggshells.

The chef used a large needle to tap a hole in the end of an egg and then suck out the contents. Tolson writes that the procedure was tricky, but no more so than getting the slips of papers with Caron's message inside the shells. Then when the waiter delivered the customer his check, he left one of the eggs in the manner that Chinese fortune cookies are served up today.

Columnist Tolson recounts that Caron was neither tactful nor a great thinker. The messages not only were outrageous, but often offended the diner. Soon customers began throwing the eggs at Caron without bothering to open them, and thus the tradition was introduced to San Antonio. When some sponsors of Fiesta events discovered that the gullible would actually pay money for the eggs if they were filled with confetti instead of messages, they began making and selling them.

Tolson's brag that *cascarones* thus originated in the Alamo City makes good reading, but it's not quite accurate. Historians have traced it back to Renaissance Italy, where the first *cascarones* were filled with scented talcum powder. From there they migrated to Spain, then Emperor Maximilian (who ruled Mexico for France for a while) and his wife, Carlotta, introduced them to Mexico City. Nobody knows for sure when they showed up in San Antonio, but the Mexican leaders who took asylum here during their country's 1910 revolt used *cascarones* to help celebrate holidays.

The Breakfast of 6,000 Eggs

For years, they have been a financial boon for Fiesta. To make sure that plenty are available for the celebration, a group of volunteer women meets every other Thursday morning beginning in September to prepare *cascarones* for sale the next April. Their principal source of supply for the eggshells is the Rodeo Cowboy Breakfast staged at the opening of the Stock Show each February. To make sure the eggs are cracked properly and the innards removed so as not to cause more than a tiny opening in the shell, the SACS ladies volunteer for the job of opening 6,000 eggs. They preserve these shells, plus those which members save throughout the year at their homes.

Many members of the society serve only scrambled eggs at home so the shells can be retained virtually intact for future *cascarones*. Once the shells are dry, each has to be filled with colored confetti, also furnished by the SACS volunteers, and a piece of thin paper glued over the opening. They are colored by conventional Easter egg dye or with scraps of colored crepe paper, so that when Fiesta begins funsters have plenty of ready ammunition.

Introduction by *Cascaron*

One use of the *cascaron* at Fiesta is to provide a way for boy to meet girl — a custom also borrowed from Mexico. There it is the tradition in the smaller communities for single women and their chaperones and single men to meet at dusk on the town plaza, where they are introduced and allowed to dance. At one point they form two circles, one inside the other. The men on the outside dance clockwise while the women inside go the other direction. Either the men or the women will have *cascarones* and usually will have secretly selected their partners. When the music stops, the one holding the *cascaron* will rush to the chosen individual and try to be the first to crack it over his/her head. The most popular girl is always the one with the most confetti in her hair.

A Memorial Procession

While the *cascaron* is in evidence at almost every Fiesta activity, it is rarely seen at the one which emphasizes most what the celebration is all about. That distinction is reserved for the solemn pilgrimage to the Alamo sponsored by the Daughters of the Republic of Texas. Since 1925, it has been staged on the Monday following April 21 — the date on which Houston and his Texan Army defeated the Mexicans at San Jacinto.

As Fiesta events go, this is one of the smallest yet most impressive. Usually from 500 to 1,000 gather at Auditorium Circle, then walk to Alamo Plaza for a benediction and to hear the 5th U.S. Army Band play taps. As the names of the 189 men who gave their lives are read aloud, each member of the procession places a wreath or a single flower at the entrance to the old mission. It is a poignant moment that recalls the real significance of Fiesta to all of Texas.

For 100 years, Fiesta parades have played to standing room only crowds. This mass of people gathered in, on and around the Majestic Theater in 1947 to watch the Battle of Flowers.

— San Antonio Light *Collection,*
Institute of Texan Cultures

Before the days of the Emergency Medical Service, U.S. Army ambulances were placed at strategic intervals along the routes of Fiesta parades to take care of any eventuality.

San Antonio Express/News *Collection,*
Institute of Texan Cultures

Harley Sadler was among Texas' best-known entertainers during the 1930s. His traveling ten theater, billed as "Harley Sadler and His Own Company," was an annual contributor to the cultural life of San Antonio and his band was a welcome addition to Fiesta parades.

— *Lewison Studio, San Antonio Museum*
Association Collection

This post card is one of the oldest photos extant of an early Battle of Flowers Parade featuring an automobile covered with posies.

Fiesta San Antonio Commission

14

All This, and Problems Too

"Everybody, soon or late, sits down to a banquet of consequences."
— **Robert Louis Stevenson**

Monarchies, both real and make-believe, have a history of disagreements. Most often these result from territorial disputes between rulers or the efforts of upstarts to put another individual on the throne. The royal "kingdom" of Fiesta is no exception.

Fiesta's problems did not begin, as some argue, with the request of Logan Stewart, El Rey Feo XXXII, to stage his own parade in 1980. As might be expected in any large organization made up primarily of volunteers, there always has been some minor dissension both internally and externally. In fact, the first intramural arguments go back to 1896, when San Antonio society objected to the selection of beautiful Austinite Ida Archer as Queen.

The choice of a "foreigner" from Austin to occupy the throne brought scathing editorial denunciations from both the *San Antonio Express* and the *Light*. Among the members of the Battle of Flowers, there also was considerable disaffection with the choice. Years later, in her *History of the Battle of Flowers Association*, Mary Etta McGimsey would write: "There followed one of the most famous battles connected with the Battle of Flowers, as many felt that with all of Miss Archer's beauty and charm, the honor should have gone to a young lady whose home was San Antonio."

The squabbles have not been limited to the organization that created Fiesta, however. There was a long-standing rivalry between the two exclusive "brother" organizations, the Order of the Alamo and the Texas Cavaliers, which John Carrington created. The Order of the Alamo is the senior group, preceding by seventeen years the formation of the Cavaliers. Since both came into being, however, there has always existed some duplication of

membership. Many of those selected as King Antonio by the Cavaliers also have belonged to the Order of the Alamo.

Nevertheless, as Henry Graham wrote in 1976 in his definitive *History of the Texas Cavaliers:* "Despite — or perhaps because of — this, a curious sibling rivalry developed between the two which persisted through the third Cavalier decade."

Business Clothes Only for His Majesty

Although Carrington himself considered the Cavaliers "in a sense complementary to the Order of the Alamo," a sub-rosa dispute existed between the two groups. Graham wrote that none of the Cavalier Kings took part in any functions of the Order of the Alamo before World War II. An early suggestion that the Order's Coronation of the Queen include both monarchs was rejected fourteen years before the Cavaliers were even organized. Even after the Cavaliers were entrusted with choosing the King, the monarch was welcome at the crowning of Her Highness only if he appeared in civilian dress and not his royal uniform.

Graham writes that this estrangement ended in 1956 and 1957 because of the efforts of John H. White and Gilbert Wright, who were members of both organizations. At their suggestion, the Queen and the Princess were invited to accompany the King on some of his school and hospital visits — a routine procedure today. The Order of the Alamo president became an honored guest at the King's Ball given by the Cavaliers. Now King Antonio not only appears in uniform at the Queen's Coronation, but his arrival is heralded by ruffles and flourishes. Frequently, both the King and Queen appear jointly at a variety of Fiesta events.

Thus while the Alamo's Queen and the Cavaliers' King still represent a royal dichotomy, relations between the two thrones have become cordial. Even El Rey Feo, the Ugly King, has an important role in Fiesta.

Other Groups Also Demanded Change

The Order of the Alamo-Cavalier rivalry was only one evidence of discontent among Fiesta participants. Many felt that the event lacked both a definite focus and centralized direction. Some efforts, only partially successful over the years, have tried to correct this.

Early on, when the celebration had grown too large for the Battle of Flowers women to manage on their own, the Chamber of Commerce had assumed a modicum of responsibility. The Chamber board attempted to coordinate the planning of all events and selected the King, usually the first businessman to ante up a $1,500 gift. Later the management was passed on to a volunteer group known as the Spring Carnival Association.

When that organization gave up its responsibility, it was replaced on May 26, 1943, by still another group — the Fiesta San Jacinto Association. However, this also did not end the discontent which grew with each passing year among those responsible for staging the event. The historian of the Cavaliers recalled that that organization's alliance with the Fiesta San Jacinto Association was "an uneasy one almost from the beginning."

It worsened as time went by. As related in a previous chapter, events finally led in 1959 to the resignation of the Cavaliers from the Fiesta San Jacinto Association. Other disgruntled participants would follow suit.

One of those, the Battle of Flowers Association, long had shared the Cavaliers' concern about the direction of Fiesta. Mrs. McGimsey, in her history of the BOFA, wrote: "Year by year there had been an increasing discontent in the week's celebration, principally because of the undemocratic procedures of a few. Representatives of a majority of the groups concerned appealed to the Chamber of Commerce as a non-participating agency to monitor a solution to the problem."

Fiesta Gets New Management

Matters came to a head following the 1959 Fiesta. Each of the major groups responsible for Fiesta — the Battle of Flowers Association, Cavaliers, German Club, Order of the Alamo, and the Junior Chamber of Commerce — quit the San Jacinto Association. These groups then took the lead, with Chamber of Commerce help, in reorganizing Fiesta management for again another time. Anxious to preserve the traditions of the organization (then sixty-eight years old), they chartered the present Fiesta San Antonio Commission, Inc. Since then, this commission has made all Fiesta policy.

Creation of the new Fiesta San Antonio Commission, Inc., although welcomed by most of the participants in the annual event, did not immediately satisfy the city's Hispanic population.

San Antonio was, is, and likely ever shall be a "Mexican town." Selected in 1718 as a mission site by Spanish Roman Catholic *padres*, then settled and made a municipality by Canary Islanders in 1731 and a province of Mexico from 1821 to 1836, San Antonio's population always has been predominantly Spanish-speaking. Even with the later influx of Anglos, Germans, Czechs, Lebanese, and at least twenty-five other ethnic groups, the latest census shows that about half of its residents are Hispanic.

The population mix was not an issue when the first Battle of Flowers was presented in 1891. The Southern aristocrats and wealthy Germans who conceived that first parade intentionally made it an exclusive, high society event. All were invited to enjoy, but mostly from the sidelines. Active participation was reserved for members of the tightly knit, clannish elite. It was, in a word, intended to be the event of the year for the upper class.

The Long History of Mexican Celebrations

Although they remained silent, for the most part, there was a feeling of resentment among much of the population toward this *nuevo fiesta*. For a century and a half before the first Battle of Flowers, similar events had been arranged and enjoyed by the greater Spanish and Mexican society. More than a century before the first Battle of Flowers, the citizens of San Antonio had, as related earlier, staged a weeklong *fiesta* to celebrate the coronation of a real monarch, Ferdinand VI of Spain.

In the 1820s, the elite among Mexican society had organized public holidays. The wealthier citizens arranged and paid for the celebrations, which were mostly religious holidays. They included street parades and always climaxed with a great ball. Attendance at the latter event was limited to the rich and prominent, but there also was another dance at the same time which was for everyone.

Through the decades, observances of special holidays continued, but were separated on the calendar from Fiesta San Antonio. They were open to all, but generally were avoided by Anglos and other non-Hispanic ethnic groups. Cinco de Mayo (May 5), the event that traditionally celebrates the Mexican struggle against an invasion by the French in 1862, has been observed for more than a century here, and *Diez y Seis de Septiembre* (September 16), Mexican Independence Day, is a spectacular commemoration spread over an entire week. The latter rivals, on a smaller scale, Fiesta itself in continuous entertainment, pageants, and dances.

Another is *El Dia de los Muertos*, the Day of the Dead, which falls on November 2. A sacred observance that dates back to the Aztecs, it's an occasion when Mexicans gather at the graves of their loved ones. There, with music, spicy foods, flowers, drink and the laughter of children, they hope to entice the shadowless souls of the dead from the Great Beyond. Mexicans believe that death is to be mocked, not feared, and they celebrate to take its power away.

The Parade of the Ugly King

With a heritage of such festivals, it is understandable why the Hispanics of San Antonio resented being only observers at Fiesta. That's why, as related in an earlier chapter, they decided to elect their own El Rey Feo, "The Ugly King," in 1947. However, it was not until thirty-three years later that the Ugly King got his own parade.

In the ensuing years, LULAC would give up its El Rey Feo Parade and assume responsibility for Fiesta Flambeau, the parade that attracts national attention because it is one of the largest illuminated night parades in the country. Under the inspired leadership of the Fiesta San Antonio Commission, feuding between the participating organizations ended. The two Kings made public appearances together and traded compliments and medals. Fiesta had become an all-San Antonio celebration.

This was the tenor of things in 1988 when Manuel (Nick) Garza, a prominent San Antonio caterer, was crowned El Rey Feo XL. Garza, like many of his predecessors on the Ugly King's throne, was a monarch with a cause. He was dedicated to education and proud of LULAC's successful scholarship program. However, there was a move within the organization itself to force his abdication and the withdrawal of LULAC from any participation in Fiesta.

LULAC Goes to Court to Dethrone a King

The problem began when Jose Garcia de Lara, president of the National League of United Latin American Citizens, questioned the way in which the local LULAC Council No. 2 was handling the scholarship funds raised by the El Rey Feo election. He ordered the dissolution of the San Antonio Council and its scholarship foundation and the assumption of the Fiesta Flambeau Parade by the national organization.

The Fiesta Commission refused the latter demand. Roger Flores, then the commission president and a former Ugly King himself, explained that Fiesta policy requires it to work only with local non-profit groups. De Lara retaliated by ordering Garza to turn in his uniform and not participate in any 1989 Fiesta functions. His directive also barred all previous Ugly Kings and those associated with their reigns from any official participation in Fiesta functions. His mandate said that "they can go as individuals. They can't wear Rey Feo regalia."

To enforce his order, De Lara asked the 166th District Court to issue a temporary injunction against such participation. Judge Peter Michael Curry who, like many other Anglos, had occupied the Ugly King throne himself in 1965, refused. This caused LULAC to question whether Judge Curry should have heard the case in the first place.

The basis of LULAC's argument concerned the policy of the Fiesta Commission in subsidizing the various events like Fiesta Flambeau. Like the Battle of Flowers and the River Parade, Flambeau has never been a profit-making enterprise. Since the three parades are among the largest and most popular events, the commission provides a partial subsidy to the sponsors of each. Under Fiesta rules, however, the sponsoring organizations have to pick up any deficits not covered by the subsidy.

Scholarships vs. Parade Deficits

LULAC officials, however, contended that the subsidies have not been distributed equitably. According to the commission executive vice-president, Marleen Pedroza, Flambeau received a $55,000 subsidy in 1989, only $10,000 less than the one to the Battle of Flowers, which is more expensive to produce. The River Parade received only $6,000. Flambeau's deficits for the 1987, 1988, and 1989 parades reached more than $40,000. LULAC argued that its Council No. 2 made up the red ink from its scholarship monies and thus was a misuse of funds.

The legal hassle resulted in an unexpected bonus for Fiesta 1989. Because Ugly King Nick Garza ignored the orders of LULAC officials and appeared as usual at the various events, his throne gained new stature with his subjects. Crowds shouted *"Viva El Rey Feo!"* when he arrived for the River Parade, and LULAC threatened not to let El Rey Feo ride on their float. King Antonio LXVII Stanton P. Bell, Jr., not only shared the spotlight with the Ugly King, but invited Garza to ride with him on the royal barge in the River Parade another "first" for the monarch that once was ignored by the socially elite.

El Rey Feo Still Has His Throne

Despite the controversies and lawsuits, the throne of El Rey Feo appears safe. Most of the points of disagreement between LULAC and the Fiesta Commission have been resolved. Fiesta Flambeau, which caused the fuss, was handed over in 1990 to a new group of sponsors, and LULAC no longer needs to be concerned about deficits the parade may incur. Perhaps most surprising of all — at least, to LULAC — was an ironic postscript to the whole affair.

While the national publicity obviously damaged LULAC's image in some quarters, it proved a bonanza to the project dearest to the organization's heart — the raising of scholarship funds for deserving Hispanic students. The media attention not only raised El Rey Feo to a higher status than he had ever enjoyed before, but it helped the candidates for the kingship to raise a record amount of money for education.

The months of colorful confusion were a blessing to Fiesta too. It demonstrated that the city's biggest bash finally had evolved into an event that belonged to all who call San Antonio home.

 **15**

The People Who Make It Happen

"The highest and best form of efficiency is the spontaneous cooperation of a free people."
— Bernard Baruch

Few cities in America could produce an event comparable to Fiesta San Antonio.

Many have rivers that are wider, longer, and more beautiful than the little stream that bisects this city. Several have tourist attractions as famous as the Alamo. According to the latest census, there are ten that are larger in size and several that are more affluent. Dozens have festivals, fiestas, jubilees, and carnivals that are outstanding and a few that are even memorable.

What, then, makes Fiesta San Antonio unique, and has for one hundred years? What is it that brings up to 800,000 people to watch the three major parades? In a city boasting hundreds of restaurants representing a smorgasbord of world menus, what induces 100,000 to pack into tiny La Villita to try fifteen different ethnic foods in the twenty hours that A Night in Old San Antonio is open?

An intangible something known locally as "the fiesta spirit" is part of it. The late Margaret Tobin, for many years the arbiter of San Antonio society, put it this way: "In Dallas, women love their clothes. In Houston, they love their homes' fine appointments. And in San Antonio, they love to have a good time. It's a fiesta city, really."

That it truly is a "fiesta city" is due, in part, to its Hispanic heritage and its polyglot population of descendants of immigrants from Europe, Asia, Central America, and the aristocracy of the Old South. Somehow this mixture produced a special chemistry, a unique environment, the aura and feeling of a place — what the Spanish call *ambiente*.

It is an *ambiente* that cuts across all social lines and includes those from every economic status. At Fiesta one finds those listed in the social register working alongside their cooks or gardeners or gas station attendants to make it all happen. And work together they do. In a given year, more than 50,000 citizens, *all volunteers*, are involved.

The Charter Says It All

The real purpose of Fiesta, expressed in somewhat flowery words, is contained in the charter it received from the State of Texas in 1959:

To encourage and help perpetuate in the minds of the people, near and far, the glorious history of Texas and the memory of the men and women who so valiantly and with great sacrifice and glory explored, settled and obtained the independence of Texas and to honor, in particular, the heroes of the Alamo, and, to this end, to promote, encourage, aid, assist and coordinate the holding of celebrations, fiestas and other events, within and without the historic City of San Antonio during the week of April 21st and at such other times during each year as may be appropriate: To encourage the study of history and culture of Texas and Latin America: to cultivate and enhance the importance of San Antonio as the meeting place or confluence of the great Anglo and Latin American cultures; and to encourage Pan American friendliness, understanding and solidarity.

This is the charge to the Fiesta San Antonio Commission, Inc., the organization responsible for the operation and continued success of the celebration. How they accomplish this with a full-time paid staff of only four people is a modern miracle of good planning.

The secret is the mobilization of one of the nation's largest volunteer battalions. Virtually everybody — from the ladies who, after a century, still stage the Battle of Flowers, to the San Antonio high school students who follow the horses in the parades as "pooper scoopers" — performs their tasks for the fun of it and the love of Fiesta.

A Business That Grosses $10 Million Per Day

Even with one out of every twenty of San Antonio's citizens actively involved in planning, producing, and executing Fiesta (and some work on it the entire year), it is a gargantuan job. It's also big business. From their small offices on St. Paul's Square near the heart of downtown, the Fiesta Commission and its staff plan and execute an event that directly pours more than $100 million into the San Antonio economy during these ten days of frivolity. Another estimated $140 million is generated indirectly into the local economy.

The commission accomplishes this on an annual budget of only $850,000, about what it costs for one day's shooting of some modern motion pictures. Not many movies, or other entertainment events, produce a return of almost 500 percent on the investment — a financial feat that has become almost routine for the planners of Fiesta San Antonio.

Fiesta is governed by the eighty-plus organizations that make up its membership. The commission has total responsibility for all aspects of the annual celebration. The planning and day-to-day operations are entrusted to a fourteen-member Executive Committee selected from the membership. From the beginning, strong ties were forged between the commission and the Greater San Antonio Chamber of Commerce. For some years, the by-laws of the organization required that the names of officers and members of the Executive Committee be approved by the Board of Directors of the Chamber.

Today the status of the Fiesta San Antonio Commission is so secure with its membership that the Chamber no longer is concerned about who is selected as officers and members of the powerful Executive Committee. The commission has proved over more than three decades that it can manage the planning and execution of what has been called "the greatest show in Texas" without having another agency looking over its shoulders.

The Fiesta San Antonio Commission is self-supporting. Member organizations pay annual dues ranging from $25 to $10,000, depending on what their involvement is and the amount of revenue it will produce for the group. In exchange, they are granted the rights to operate activities ranging from events like A Night in Old San Antonio to selling seats for the parades and running concession stands. Organizations which take no profit from their Fiesta activities pay $100 annually.

The commission has other sources of income too. The downtown carnival is a major one. It is estimated by Phil Sheridan, who has operated the event for the commission since 1973, that about 800,000 people pass through the gate each year. As a result, the show produces more than thirty percent of the commission's budget. San Antonians love the carnival and support it generously. It gives downtown a village air with its one-hundred-foot-tall ferris wheel, as many as forty other rides, an equal number of games, and a score of food booths scattered through a six-block area. These amenities make up for the traffic snarls caused by the blocking of traffic on key business streets.

Charities Benefit from Fiesta

Although the thousands of seats for the river and street parades are sold by charitable, civic, patriotic, and similar organizations for their own benefit, they buy their permits and rent the chairs from the commission. A souvenir program issued for each Fiesta is heavily subsidized by advertisers. The dozens of stands selling *raspa,* those syrup-drenched balls of ice shavings in a paper cup, operate in the summer around Alamo Plaza. During Fiesta, however, they and other concessionaires have to buy permits from the commission. In recent years, the sale of television rights to the three major parades has become a new source of income. Also, the Fiesta Commission operates a gift shop during the annual celebration which sells a variety of souvenir items.

The biggest money-maker for a single organization is the Conservation Society's Night in Old San Antonio. It grosses more than $1.5 million on four successive nights and the profits are invested in the society's historical preservation projects. La Semana Alegre, sponsored by the Junior Chamber of commerece, is another event whose entertainment, food, and dancing is a successful generator of funds for worthy causes.

Altogether there are some 150 separate events in the ten days of Fiesta. The majority, including the three big parades and all of the smaller ones, are free. Participants range from toddlers (as in the Shoe Box Parade) to senior citizens who now have their own special events. Coordinating it all is the Fiesta Commission and its tiny staff.

Meetings of the Fiesta San Antonio Commission, the group responsible for planning and directing the annual event, are usually serious but they can be fun too. Here the members are decked out in "crazy hats" for a contest.

— Al Rendon

A Ten-Day Job That Lasts 365 Days

When Fiesta began as the Battle of Flowers a century ago, the responsibility for staging it fell largely on the shoulders of one woman, Mrs. H. D. Kampmann. She was named chairman.

Today the primary responsibility once again rests with a woman. She is Marleen Pedroza, the executive vice-president of the Fiesta San Antonio Commission. A veteran of the commission staff, she was named to the top position in 1983, when Davis Burnett, who had held the paid position since 1969, resigned.

Over the years, the leadership position has had a variety of titles and has been held by many different individuals. Sometimes it has been a paid job and sometimes it has been a labor of love.

Today, as the highest-ranking full-time paid staff member of the commission, Ms. Pedroza is the administrator charged with planning, sanctioning, and coordinating every aspect of the event. As the behind-the-scenes executive, she has made it a policy to learn as much as possible about similar entertainments by visiting them. Her status in the field has been recognized by her election as president of the International Festivals Association.

Like most San Antonians, Marleen Pedroza is certain that Fiesta San Antonio will still be going strong — and still growing — a hundred years from now. That's because there is so much community involvement — more, she believes, than in any similar celebration in America. As Margaret Tobin observed, San Antonio really is "a city of *fiesta*" and likely ever shall be.

Getting Ready for the 1990 Court of Artistic Splendour

One of the most important assignments is that of Mistress of the Robes for the Coronation of the Order of the Alamo Queen. The job can begin as long as two years before the Coronation for which the Mistress is responsible. In charge of robes for the 1990 Coronation was Mrs. Hugh Halff, Jr., shown here playing make-believe with the crown the new Queen will wear.

Every Fiesta Court, especially one of Artistic Splendour, requires a talented artist. Here artist Zelime Matthews shows Duchess Amy McFarlane and her mother, Jane, a design for the robe she will wear in the Coronation.

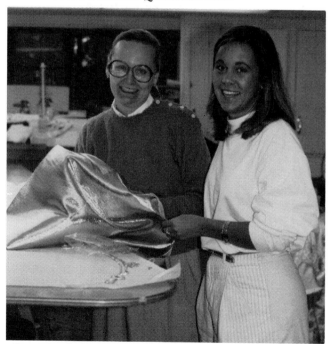

Once the design is approved, the fabrics have to be selected. Here Duchess Francie Steves does that with the help of Clara Chumney, dressmaker.

Long sessions of fitting begin many weeks before the Coronation. Duchess Roxana Seeligson is shown being measured by her dressmaker, Terry Brantley.

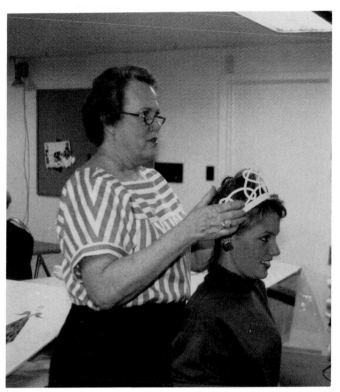

Crowns and tiaras are the order of the evening when the Order of the Alamo crowns its Queen. Duchess Kathryn Johnston is fitted here by Billee Hare, the official maker of head pieces for the Coronation.

Ardyce Erickson, dressmaker, shows Duchess Elizabeth Middleton the progress on her gown as her parents, Barbra and Fred Middleton, watch.

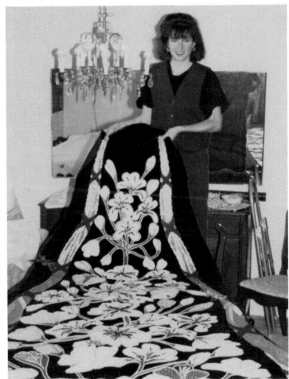

Queen Linda McSween of the 1990 Court of Artistic Splendour examines her train for final approval.

Queen Linda tries on her royal gown at a final fitting while her father, Paul McSween, looks on approvingly.

Above: Robes for the Queen of the Cornyation, unlike those that adorn the Order of the Alamo's Queen, are designed to spoof royalty.

— Al Rendon

Below: Bicycles have been a part of Fiesta since the first Battle of Flowers in 1891. Then they were decorated with flowers. Today they're racing bikes.

— Fiesta San Antonio Commission

MEMBERS OF THE FIESTA SAN ANTONIO COMMISSION — 1990

Academy of Health Sciences
Agudas Achim
Air Force 12th Flying Training Wing
Air Force Military Training Center
Air Training Command
Alamo City Bowlers
Alamo City Rugby Football Club
Alamo Square and Round Dance Association
Alamo Volleyball Association
Alpha Pi Zeta Chapter, Zeta Phi Beta Sorority
Army 90th Reserve Command
Army Health Services Command
Baptist Memorial Hospital System
Battle of Flowers Association
Beethoven Maennerchor
Brooke Army Medical Center
Brooks Air Force Base
Central Park Merchants Association
Confederation of Charros of San Antonio
Daughters of the Republic of Texas, Alamo Mission
    Chapter
El Consejo de Reyes Feos Anteriores
Electronic Security Command
Fiesta Del Mercado
Fiesta Flambeau Parade Association
Fifth Recruiting Brigade, Southwest
Fifth United States Army
Fort Sam Houston
Grand Lodge, Sons of Herman
Incarnate Word College
Kelly Air Force Base
King William Association
Lackland Air Force Base
Ladies of Charissa
LULAC Council #2
Marine Corps Reserve
Military-Civilian Club (C)
Military-Civilian Club (M)
Miss Fiesta San Antonio Scholarship Pageant, Inc.
Miss San Antonio Scholarship Pageant
North Star Mall Merchants Association
Order of the Alamo
Our Lady of the Lake University

Paseo del Rio Association
Perry-Gething Foundation
Queen of Soul
Randolph Air Force Base
Randolph Art League
Retired Senior Volunteer Program
River Art Group
Rotary Clubs of San Antonio
San Antonio Air Logistics Center
San Antonio Area, Council of Girl Scouts
San Antonio Bicycle Racing Club
San Antonio Cactus and Xerophyte Society
San Antonio Chamber of Commerce
San Antonio Chapter, American Red Cross
San Antonio Chapter, Knights of Columbus
San Antonio Charro Association
San Antonio Conservation Society
San Antonio German Club
San Antonio Hispanic Chamber of Commerce
San Antonio Jaycees
San Antonio Lacrosse Club
San Antonio Little Theater
San Antonio Museum Association
San Antonio Road Runners
San Antonio Symphony Society
San Antonio Women's Soccer Association
San Antonio Zoological Society
San Antonio Zulu Association
San Fernando Cathedral
Society for the Preservation of Historic Fort Sam
    Houston
Sons of the Republic of Texas
Southwest Craft Center
State Association of Texas Pioneers
St. Luke's Festival Association
St. Mary's University
St. Mary's University Alumni Association
Texas Army National Guard
Texas Cavaliers
Trinity University
University of Texas at San Antonio
University of Texas Health Science Center
United States Navy
University of Texas Institute of Texan Cultures
Woman's Club of San Antonio

SAN ANTONIO, TEXAS, TUESDAY MORNING, APRIL 21, 1891

HARRISON, THE SECOND

Visits San Antonio and is tendered an ovation in the rain

A GALA DAY UNDER SOME DIFFICULTIES BUT PLEASANT WITHALL

Ben and Wanny and Jerry all Talk and Make Remarks that are Very Nice Indeed

A PROCESSION IN THE RAIN WITHOUT THE LADIES

The Reception at the Opera House a Crush of the Happenings and By-Plays of the Day Notices and Incidents

In consummation of at least a week's expectancy, Benjamin Harrison, president of the United States, arrived in San Antonio at 9:15 o'clock yesterday morning. At an early hour a crowd of anxious citizens and visitors gathered at the Sunset depot and took their stations to await the incoming of the first class train on which the president and his party were comfortably ensconced. Thus in, this motley crowd . . . presented a scene well worth gazing upon. Here was a cluster of ladies, securely wrapped, chatting pleasantly and on the qui vive to get a glimpse of Mrs. Harrison's bonnet; a little further on were several members of the Grand Army of the Republic dutifully badged and buttoned,

while the colored brother was also in great number, evidently intent upon a view of the chief representative of a great party. Prominent gentlemen of this and other places were mingling in the crowd, while the reception composed of twelve or more leading citizens was in readiness the moment to greet the president and to extend the courtesies and the freedom of the city.

And so the crowd waited in the rain and slush to do homage to the chief executive of the Union. An eager, expectant look was on the face of each, and every jingle of a car bell, or scream of an engine, would strike a pulse in the crowd which caused a rush for a good view and a position for a handshake. And they waited, and the rain fell, and the mud grew thicker and firmer. At 9:10 o'clock a whistle was heard up the road and in a few moments the presidential pilot engine came puffing up the slope, decorated with flags, flowers and bunting. The crowd rushed to the platform, all craned their necks, the pilot engine gave warnings for a clear track and the special train came rolling in amidst loud hurrahs and a bountiful supply of cooling rain. At 9:15 o'clock the engine wheels were stationary and President Benjamin Harrison and party were in San Antonio.

The presidential train consisted of five coaches drawn by engine No. 622. The distinguished party consisted of President Harrison and Mrs. Benjamin Harrison, Postmaster General Wannamaker, Secretary of Agriculture Rusk, Mrs. McKee, Mrs. Russell Harrison, Mrs. Dimmick and Mrs. Boyd. Accompanying the party were Alfred J. Clark, Associated Press correspondent, Oscar P. Austin, of the

Press News association, and Richard V. Oulsbain, of the United Press.

As the presidential train slowed up at the depot, there was a momentary lull in the excitement of the crowd and the long row of cars was eagerly scanned to catch a view of the president and members of his cabinet. This silence was but for a moment. The crowd was satisfied that the president was really and actually in its midst though temporarily hid from view. An outburst of loud cheers gave immediate vent to its feelings and it surged up alongside the cars on each side of the track. The side doors of the vestibule at the front end of the rear coach were opened as the train came to a standstill and the deputation of San Antonio ladies first entered the car. This deputation was composed of Mesdames D. S. Stanley, W. J. R. Patterson, C. C. Creason, and C. K. Brenneman. When these ladies had been safely piloted through the wet and rain under cover of the umbrellas of the reception committee, the latter passed into the magisterial presence to single file. Prominent among this committee were Messrs. Hon. Bryan Callaghan, S. M. Johnson, Colonel C. M. Terrell, Reagan Houston, W. J. B. Patterson, Charles Hugo, J. S. Lockwood, Dr. J. P. Oroelsa, H. D. Kampmann, Dr. Amos Graves, W. N. Mason, J. S. Alexander and C. K. Brenneman.

The scene inside the car was sufficient to make even the most radical democrat enthusiastic. In the center of the coach stood the president, surrounded by the members of his party. He looked dignified and his face bore a pleasant,

CONTINUED ON NEXT PAGE

though somewhat fatigued, expression. As each member of the committee stepped forward with some cordial word of greeting and grasped the president's hand, he replied in a way that showed his sincere appreciation of the genuineness of his reception. Everyone seemed to be in a happy mood and not the slightest trace of restraint was manifested to either the visitors or the citizens. A few minutes sufficed for all introductions and the visitors stood in little knots chatting freely and exchanging ideas. The interior of the car while in no sense gorgeous were costly furnished and a wealth of flowers in bouquets and ornamental designs imparted a delicious freshness and color to its appearance, while shedding a distinct and most agreeable fragrance. The mahogany woodwork of the car was highly polished and the roof was inlaid with various woods. Scattered here and there were easy chairs, upholstered in rich colored velvet. The whole effect of being at once pleasing and artistic.

General D. S. Stanley, who was in full undress uniform, had accompanied the president from Galveston and he now inquired if the president was desirous of carrying out the program that had been arranged. President Harrison on conferring with the ladies of his party, decided to at once place himself at the disposal of the reception committee. The ladies, however, decided to remain on board the cars, as the heavy torrents of rain bespoke little pleasure in sightseeing. A move was then made to the rear of the train. The platform here was of unusual size and staply protected from the rain. As President Harrison stepped out of the door to the platform a muted outburst of applause from the expectant throng of spectators around the

depot brought a flush of pleasure to his face. Again and again the roof of the depot re-echoed the ringing cheers that greeted his appearance. The occasion was unusual, and all knew it. It was the first occasion of a president setting foot on the soil of the metropolis of the greatest state in the Union. A portly figure now joined the group from the interior of the car. He needed no introduction as the thousand cries of "Hogg" proved. Amid a renewed round of applause, Governor Hogg led the way to the carriages in waiting. Following the governor came President Harrison, then Postmaster General Wannamaker and Secretary of Agriculture Rusk. The rear was brought up by General S. Stanley, Major Sangery, aide-de-camp to the president, Major Bryan Callaghan and the members of the reception committee.

Outside in front of the depot the members of the Grand Army of the Republic were conspicuous in their blue uniforms and in the street was a guard of the United States Third cavalry under command of Captain Hunter. Two carriages, each drawn by four gray horses and gaily decorated with flags and laurel, stood in waiting for the presidential party. These carriages were at once entered and the members of the various committees and unattached citizens filled many more carriages, forming quite a long procession. The destination of the party was the Grand opera house on Alamo plaza. The route taken was via Grand Avenue and Avenue D to the plaza. In the face of the tremendous downpour with its attendant mud and unpleasantness the route was not lined by as many loyal spectators as would otherwise have been the case.

At various points, however, groups of citizens stood patiently

under the shelter of great coats and umbrellas till the carriages passed. Many of the houses displayed flags and their occupants standing on the porches waved a sentiment of welcome. The change in the program at the last moments, by which the president first visited the opera house, found many people unprepared for his early arrival in the city and in consequence when the opera house was reached a full attendance of the various committees was not on the ground. Nevertheless the news that the president had arrived had caused many to be on the alert and the sidewalk approaches to the opera house were packed with citizens. A steady stream of vehicles joined the already large number in the procession and the plaza was soon filled to overflowing.

RECEPTION

The opera house was reached at 9:40 o'clock and here was stationed a large detachment of the local militia in full uniform and with fixed bayonets. As the president alighted the citizen soldiers presented arms and he was at once conducted through the theatre to the wings. The presence of the militia lent a rigidity to the proceedings and served to greatly minimalize the inconvenience of the dense mass of people that crushed into the house. Two sergeants stood with crossed bayonets at the outer doors of the auditorium and allowed the throng to pass into the house by sections.

The arrangements made by the committee for seating the audience were admirable and in a brief space of time every seat in the house was occupied. In the history of a house that has contained vast crowds on many notable occasions, there was never anything seen to approach the multitude within its doors yesterday. Every seat, every box, every passage and inch of standing room was filled. The audience was wedged together in a solid mass but no thought of discomfort — all ideas were centered on seeing and hearing the distinguished visitors. Three rows of seats had been placed on the stage and President Harrison walked to the front and acknowledged the warm greeting of an audience which was already warmed to the highest pitch of enthusiasm. Secretary Rusk and Postmaster General Wannamaker were also loudly welcomed, and a special ovation was tendered Governor Hogg.

The president occupied the centre seat of the front row. On his right sat in order Postmaster Wannamaker and Secretary Rusk; on the president's left sat Hon. Mayor Callaghan and Axel Meerscheidt, the latter representing the commercial bodies of the city. In the second row sat Major Sanger, with General D. S. Stanley and Charles Hugo on the right and C. W. Ogden, Granville Martin, H. D. Kampmann and Dr. P. Orneiss on the left. The third row was occupied by Messrs. S. M. Johnson, Dr. Amos Graves, C. K. Brenneman, Rev. Dr. Giddings, A. T. Wilson, Reagan Houston, C. C. Creason, H. F. Yoakum, Colonel C. M. Terrell and Nelson Mackey. Later in the proceedings Judge Noonan, General Young, Mayor McDonnell of Austin, L. L. Foster, land commissioner, and a number of prominent citizens and members of the Commercial Exchange occupied places on the stage.

The decorations in the opera house were not elaborate, but such as good taste might dictate. At the front of the stage where the drop curtain falls were two immense Union Jacks caught in the center and draped to loose folds on either side, the ends reaching to the

ground. A similar arrangement of flags formed the background, with the addition of a red, white, and blue streamer in the middle. Facing the proscenium in the front of the upper gallery was a banner bearing the legend: "The Lone Star state. The morning star of freedom, rivalled only by the ascending sun of the nation."

In introducing the president Mayor Callaghan in a neat speech expressed the pleasure the city had in receiving the nation's president, and he gracefully presented him to the large audience. The president said:

"Fellow citizens: I much regret that frequent speaking in the open air has greatly impaired my voice, and will not enable me to express my thanks at the cordial reception as I would like. I assure you I sympathize with you in that the day is so unpropitious, and yet I have been told that this rain is worth $5,000,000 to you. This being the case our regrets are modified. I doubtless am the cause of this downpour, and if it is really worth that much to Texas I will not ask more than one-half. It is very pleasant for me to visit this beautiful and historic city. The history has been written, and my glances must be brief, but the men of martyrdom are still fresh in your memory and the story will be told to your children.

"I remember in my early boyhood to have heard of the deeds and experiences of some who bore my name. I am glad to stand where these experiences occurred and to revive them in my memory. The stipulations and conditions in which Texas came into the Union were not such as to inspire the pride and prosperity that it now does. The great capabilities, industrial developments, climate and variety of productions, give promise

of prominence for Texas among the greatest states of the Union. You are now beginning to take up and brake with the plow, and to diversify your interests. I hope you will add a diversity of mechanical products and the cultivating of fruit and grain. Your cotton should be spun here, and I hope the people will turn their interests in this direction. Just in proportion as home industry is practiced and encouraged, so is prosperity and good of a country increased. I am surprised by the vastness of your territory, and am glad that the pride of an American is in one system of government a free, independent, order-loving people which dwells in the Union. I am glad to know you are giving more attention to education and I am pleased with your school systems. Schools are our pride and the safeguards of our nation. In the city where I dwell everybody attends the public school. It is the training of those who will take positions of prominence in our history. No material greatness or wealth is to be compared with the higher merits of our homes and the purity of our youth. All is dependent upon social order and society. Wealth and commerce are timid and still only come where God reigns and intelligence is great.

"Thanking you all for your kindness and hospitality, not stinted in the least by differences of political faith. I must beg you to excuse me from further speaking. I am in the hands of your committee and will take pleasure in getting as well acquainted with you as our plans admit."

THE POSTMASTER GENERAL

Hon. C. W. Ogden next introduced Postmaster General Wannamaker, who addressed the people. He said:

"Mr. Mayor: I can not speak the pleasure I have in coming in under this umbrella and in having this visit. When people walk under this rain umbrella they get well acquainted, and this, you know, is what we want. It seems on this trip that we have been half the time in getting through Texas.

"Why, you have to get up early in the morning to walk around your governor! You will have to get Secretary Rusk, who has, or will have charge of the weather, and is giving us a nice little touch now, to behave better towards you. But this grand and truly hospitable reception just shows what you could do if given a chance and impresses upon us the fact that no storm or rain can beat out the enthusiasm of your hearts. Though under unpropitious circumstances of wind and weather, we take great pleasure in meeting our bosses. Mr. Rusk is much interested in your agricultural development and is planting pumpkins all over the country. I am just as industrious and am planting post offices. I find that they grow well in Texas soil. Your state has asked for as many as any in the Union and it got all it wanted. The government belongs as much to Texas as to Maine or Ohio, and if you don't get what you want it is because you don't ask for it. We will go back with greater desires to lift up this great state of yours, in which this rain is falling and wishing your state the highest prosperity. It will not be long before steamers will be carrying your commuters and mail to every nation. I am more interested in this latter than to manufacturing your own cotton. Indeed, if you should follow the president's advice it will become very lonesome in New England . . . will have to move those states down into Texas. You are entitled to all you want and in two or

three years visitors will see greater resources and more magnificent buildings. I rejoice that we are on the doorstep of an era of greater prosperity. The man who thinks that all the opportunities are gone is mistaken. I believe we are standing in the open door of a golden age; I believe your open hands extended to the brothers of the north will bring them and your minds will be opened, your rails built up and a great manufacturing enthusiasm will be built up. Oh, for one heart, one flag, one nation, that when prosperity comes to the north the south can rejoice, and when southern victory is crowned, that the north can throw up its hat and join in the tidings of great joy, and we all stand for the general good. We are now working out the scheme of government, opening up new marts and joining hands for future success. I trust the day is not far distant when we shall have postal savings banks to easy reach of home, where the poor man can save to buy a house.

"Standing at a distance and reading the newspapers, one would suppose it a very handsome thing, only an hour or two of work, to be connected with the government, but this is an injustice. There is more zealous, sacrificing work than one would think but all in our power, whatever comes under our province, will be done irrespective of party and for the general good. In taking leave of you, I thank you for this beautiful welcome you have given the president on this gala day."

THE SECRETARY'S SPEECH

General Stanley paid a happy tribute introducing Secretary Rusk, who spoke as follows:

"Fellow citizens: I am glad to meet you here, if in the rain. Postmaster General Wannamaker has

made all the wet speeches on this trip and has not left anything for me to say. I don't know what he would have done about his speech if it had not rained. He remarks that we have been traveling half the time on this trip in Texas. That is so, and when we get through I want to come right back again. He was talking about walking around your governor. Don't walk around him; walk square up to him. I like his looks and, as the fellow said, the way his clothes hang on him. This party has its objects: the president draws the crowd, Wannamaker entertains it and I disperse them."

THE GOVERNOR'S TALK

The mayor arose to introduce Governor Hogg, but a voice from the rear was heard, "He doesn't need any introduction, let him fire away." The governor expressed the gratitude he felt at the manner in which the president and his party had been received and spoke on the many ovations they had received since first they saw the State of Texas. He paid high tributes to the president and his cabinet and closed by thanking the people for their uniform courtesy and hospitality.

THE HANDSHAKING

While the echoes of the governor's speech still vibrated in the air, C. W. Ogden announced from the footlights that President Harrison would hold a brief and informal reception. This announcement again brought forth universal applause and the audience rose to its feet and pressed forward to the door on the north side of the building, leading to the stage. A line was formed at the front of the stage by the militia and members of the committee, and before this passed a constant stream of people for the space of 35 minutes, each one shaking the president's hand to the grasp of friendship.

The sight was a novel one to many and it presented a most interesting spectacle.

Standing alone in front of the little speaker's table on which was draped many a choice bouquet, the chief executive of over 60,000,000 people all speaking the same tongue and animated by a loyal patriotism was engaged in making a page in the ephemeral history of a nation. Whatever might have been the politics of the crowd it was a democratic one in the broad sense of the word. There was no distinction or difference. Young and old of every color, from the fairest tint of young womanhood to the ebon-hued son of Ham. Of every grade and station the people filed past, some in rich apparel and others in plain clothing; women crippled and men in the strength of manhood, but all were alike accorded as equal welcome. Many children as they passed presented little nosegays of flowers and at the close of the event the president apparently was much moved at such a grand demonstration of patriotism.

THE DRIVE THROUGH TOWN

A start was made from the Grand opera house at 11:50 o'clock. In the first carriage were President Harrison, Governor Hogg, Mayor Callaghan, and Major Sanger. The second carriage contained Secretary Rusk, Colonel Terrell, General Stanley and C. K. Brenneman. The third carriage was occupied by Postmaster Wannamaker, S. J. Johnson, W. J. H. Patterson.

The route taken was through Crockett and Losoyo streets to Commerce street. As the carriages drove down the avenues, the presidential party had a good view of the retail commercial establish-

ments of the city. Commerce street led into Main plaza and from there to Military plaza. At this latter point the horses were again headed north, after a few moments had been spent in viewing from the carriage the new city hall building. The president and party expressed their surprise and approbation at the grandeur of the design and the suitability of the building as the city hall of the metropolis of Texas. From Military plaza the carriages again entered Commerce street and thence into St. Mary's street where in passing over the bridge the president caught a glimpse of the beauties of the San Antonio river and the magnificence of the structure spanning it at this point, on all of which he commented. St. Mary's street led into College street and from College through Navarro, Houston street was soon reached.

Here a great many groups of enthusiasts had assembled and as the procession passed the president bowed his acknowledgements from the carriage window. Avenue D was next entered and in this street the handsome dwellings and grassy lawns with trees in full leaf were noticed by the visitors. From Avenue D the Sunset depot was reached via Grand avenue and Austin street. A moment or two of delay at the depot and the string of carriages moved on to the Government post via Crosby and connecting streets to Grayson streets. A brief halt was called at the entrance to the lower parade grounds, while the guard approached and saluted. As the president's carriage passed the sentry the watches of the party showed but a few seconds wanting of noon.

His arrival within the gates was simultaneous with the first boom of the president's salute of 21 guns. Away in the distance on the grassy

parade could be seen through the drizzle the blue-cloaked artillery and with the drifting smoke the words of command of the battery officer floated towards the carriages at the end of the parade. Time was pressing, however, and if the post was to be seen it required some smart driving. The tour of pleasurable inspection was continued along the north and east sides of the parade. On the latter side, as the procession swept along, the artillery drawn up in the grass saluted their commander-in-chief. Turning out at the entrance to the quartermaster's department the road was gained and the upper parade ground was reached. The complete tour of this was made going on the north side and returning to the south. The Twenty-third Infantry band was stationed in the entrance of the castle-like front of the barracks and during the tour they played "The President's March."

In common with the many other things that were not, but might and would have been had the weather not been at fault, was the parade. The various companies and troops, however, standing in parade in front of their respective quarters, came as near to a general parade as circumstances would permit. Greated-coated and motionless, with arms at the present and subordinate officers in the center and to the front with swords aloft, the nation's defenders attracted the especial attentions of President Harris and party.

UP AND AWAY

The post survey having been concluded, the carriages returned towards the Sunset depot. To avoid the confusion and a rush likely to be met at the depot, the presidential train was switched to the south bend of the track above the depot. Here the cars were finally reached by the party. Little time was lost in getting aboard and several army officers took the opportunity and came to pay their respects to the president.

"One minute before we start," was announced by the conductor and the coaches were moved slowly down to the depot on the main line. Now came the only disagreeable moment of the whole trip. Friends of whom the presidential party had many and newly, but none the less surely formed, had to be parted with and the citizens would in a few seconds . . . the valued friends who were in their midst. The San Antonio ladies' committee would have to leave the companionship of the visiting ladies and the inviting atmosphere of the private car, to face a bleak and drizzling day and a return to old-time friends. Good byes were sincerely said. The mayor of San Antonio in a few words parted with the president, as did many others. Postmaster Johnston hesitated, with a foot on the platform steps, to impress a word on Postmaster General Wannamaker's brain. The officers saluted and withdrew and President Harrison, stepping on the rear platform, was greeted with cheer after cheer and his hand was wrung in earnest by many a citizen as he reached down over the end rail of the car.

The end had come. The signal cord gave a spasmodic jerk and the train moved westward at 12:30 o'clock exactly, to race over the boundless prairies of Western Texas. The president's visit was at an end and a few minutes later the falling drops of rain did not hit a single citizen in the neighborhood of the Sunset depot.

HOW THEY SHOOK

The various styles and methods of handshaking during the president's reception were a study for the disinterested. There was a be-

wildering variety among which was noticed at random:

The active, polished businessman, who stepped along briskly, grasped the president's hand firmly, bowed his unspoken word of recognition and resumed his way to the door.

The political man came along with quite an air of proprietorship in every look and gesture. He appeared to feel that he was quite an instrument in obtaining for the president his present position. He stepped forward, made quite a patronizing scrutiny of the president, shook the outstretched hand with an air of condescension and passed on, wondering why the president did not call him by name.

The funny man next hove in sight. He trod the floor lightly, made facial grimaces at the stewards, whom he worried with his attempts to get out of line. As he grasped the president's hand he gave a sickly grin and rushed forward in the hope of being able to propel some previous guest down the flight of three stairs at one bound.

The smiling miss was also one of the contestants for presidential recognition. She sidled along, casting simpering glances at the stewards and now and again giving them temporary palpitation of the heart as she seemed on the verge of toppling off the stage. On reaching His Nibs she would stretch out three fingers and a light glove, twist her body into a Grecian bend and, this done, slide along proudly to the door, forgetful for once of her lace dress until a ripping sound showed that it had caught to some of the property man's lumber.

The sweet little unconventional American girl nudged merrily along in the line with a little bouquet in her hands which she seemed awfully anxious to pre-

serve intact. As she got closer and closer to the central figure she would take a wondering peep at a real live president from behind those she followed. She knew no self-consciousness but looking up into the president's eyes with a smile of innocent trust playing in her eyes, she could be seen presenting her offering, shaking hands and then passing from sight.

The great colored man was perhaps the most interesting. He took up lots of room in the procession. He was not going to be crowded on such an occasion. He found himself suddenly in front of the president. His presence of mind was sorely taxed, but he did not forget to shake the extended hand. He shook it "good," as he afterwards said. Then he passed out into the world again, and no one could tell that he had shaken hands with the president.

THE PRESS NOT IN IT

In keeping with the reputation San Antonio has acquired for indifference to the wants of the press, the arrangements yesterday were characteristic. If there were any arrangements at all they were of a negative character and could not easily have been worse. Quite a number of press men, both visiting and local, were busily engaged throughout the day preparing reports which the public might criticize at leisure next day. For the accommodation or comfort of the correspondents accompanying the presidential party no one seemed to be responsible. During the meeting in the Grand opera house the president's private stenographer was obliged to take notes standing with his back to the side scenes. The Associated Press and local men had to scramble for places originally intended for committeemen and copy had to be prepared as best it might.

Whether it was intended that reporters should use the floor or not for a table is not known, but the absence of a table pointed that way. The impression produced on the visiting correspondents could not have been a pleasant one, especially after the generous reception they had received at the hands of prominent Galveston citizens. Colonel C. M. Terrell was the only person known to have made a suggestion for their comfort, but alone he was powerless.

WANNY IN THE POST OFFICE

In the interval of President Harrison's reception at the Grand opera house Postmaster General Wannamaker took occasion to visit the new federal building and post office. Accompanying the distinguished visitor were Postmaster S. M. Johnson, Colonel C. M. Terrell and W. J. B. Patterson. Postmaster Wannamaker made a minute inspection of the building from cellar to the top of the tower. From the latter point he enjoyed a birds-eye view, such as the misty rain would permit. He also shook hands and personally conversed with all the post office employees. He expressed the extreme gratification his visit had afforded him in no stinted terms. The actual building had much surpassed his most hopeful anticipations and the method and manner in which the business was conducted met with his utmost approval. The presidential party was . . . presence by-the-bye, and Wannamaker made his connection with the president on Commerce street after the opera house ceremonies.

NOTES AND PERSONALS

The ladies were quite enthusiastic over Mrs. Russell B. Harrison and they declared that she was "just too lovely for anything."

A delegation from Laredo was composed of Mayor Pro Tem L. J. Christen, Captain Dodd, R. E. Stumberg, H. Thalson, Leonard Hayes, W. Benninham and I. Polick.

A peculiar feature of the arrangements of the presidential train was the presence of a few finnicky ventilating fans. These were propelled by electricity and mounted under the roof.

There were no particular flies noticeable upon the governor, and the ovation tendered him might have led a stranger to believe that he had come all the way from Washington, too.

The reputation of San Antonio was well upheld by a knot of its prominent citizens yesterday. Of these, Colonel C. M. Terrell was conspicuous by his dignified and gentlemanly bearing.

W. J. B. Patterson was an indefatigable worker during the entire stay of the party in the city. Mrs. Patterson was also foremost in the enjoyable task of entertaining the ladies of the party.

Alfred J. Clark, the Associated Press correspondent accompanying the presidential party, is a particularly pleasing and accommodating gentleman. His brethren of the local press are indebted to him for favors received.

Dr. and Mrs. J. P. Kline joined the procession in transit to post headquarters and thence to the president's special car and presented to Mrs. Harrison in behalf of the E. O. C. Ord. Woman's Relief corps an exquisite bouquet of white flowers.

The train which brought in the presidential party made most excellent time. The distance of 216 miles was made in six hours and thirty minutes. J. K. Ryona was conductor, Walter Jordan pulled the throttle and Mike Garney yanked the brakes.

Locomotive No. 622 has often been commented on by travelers as being the most spick-and-span machine that ever snorted the breath of the exhaust pipes. Its chief officer outdid himself yesterday. If Oscar Wilde had seen it he would have composed a poem with No. 622 for the theme.

It was odd and somewhat unfortunate that the only street car encountered by the president on his carriage drive through the town should be a mule car. As the mule cars in San Antonio can be counted on the fingers of one hand the impression produced may be far from reality.

The county and district officials drove down to the depot in hacks and assisted to make things pleasant for President Harrison. Perhaps there was no more enthusiastic citizen in the number who greeted the president than the amiable County Judge McAllister, who headed the deputation.

Captain Nelson Mackey, with his characteristic thoughtfulness, presented President Harrison with a superb bouquet of Japanese lilies. He also presented Governor Hogg with a very artistic bouquet of flowers. Both the recipients of these marks of friendship expressed the keen pleasure with which the gifts were received.

The children of the public schools were sadly disappointed that the weather prevented their participating in the festivities. From the time it was first intimated that they should take part, till the battering rain awoke them they had thought and talked of little else. San Antonio has a large school population and it would have proved one of the most successful features of the reception.

A party of about thirty came over from the Capital City Sunday night to get in a glimpse of the president and see the city in gala attire. Prominent among them were Mayor McDonald, Commissioner of Agriculture Foster, W. L. McGaugher, of the land office, J. M. Boroughs, wife and daughter, Miss Margie P. Pessets, J. W. Burke, A. S. Roberts, John C. Lewis and Senator Glasscock.

Postmaster General Wannamaker would seem to have produced the most favorable impression on the citizens of any of the distinguished visitors. His bodily presence is fine and his clear-cut features and quick eye go to show a man of more than ordinary ability. His manner was particularly pleasing and those with whom he came in contact will remember his visit with much pleasure.

Bibliography

The following is not intended to be complete. Rather, it only suggests some of the major sources drawn upon in writing *A Century of Fiesta in San Antonio*.

Books

Cagle, Jr., Eldon. *Quadrangle: The History of Fort Sam Houston*. Austin: Eakin Press, 1988.
Corner, William. *San Antonio de Bexar: A Guide and History*. San Antonio: Bainbridge & Corner, 1880.
Davis, John L. *San Antonio: A Historical Portrait*. Austin: Encino Press, 1978.
Everett, Donald E. *San Antonio Legacy*. San Antonio: Trinity University Press, 1979.
———. *San Antonio: Flavor of Its Past*. San Antonio: Trinity University Press, 1975.
Graham, Henry. *A History of the Texas Cavaliers*. Published by The Cavaliers, 1976.
The Handbook of Texas. Vols. I & II. Austin: Texas State Historical Association, 1952.
House, Boyce. *City of Flaming Adventure: The Chronicle of San Antonio*. San Antonio: The Naylor Company, 1949.
McGimsey, Mary Etta. *Battle of Flowers Association of San Antonio, 1891–1966*.
New Encyclopedia of Texas. Published pre-1900.
Olmsted, Frederick Law. *A Journey Through Texas*. New York, 1857.
Order of the Alamo. *Yearbooks of the Coronations*.
Ramsdell, Charles. *San Antonio: A Historical and Pictorial Guide*. Austin: University of Texas Press, 1959.
West, John O. *Mexican-American Folklore*. Little Rock: August House, Inc., 1988.

Articles

Cruz, Gilbert R. "Habemus Regem: San Antonio Festivities on the Occasion of the Ascension of Ferdinand VI to the Spanish Crown, 1747." *Semana de las Missions*, published by Our Lady of the Lake University, 1980.
de la Tara, Jesus F., and John Wheat. "Bexar: Profile of a Tejano Community." *Southwestern Historical Quarterly of the Texas State Historical Association*, July 1985.
Maguire, Jack. "Fiesta es Ambiente." *Caminos de Aires Magazine* (Mexico City), March–April 1982.
———. "San Antonio." *Caminos de Aires Magazine* (Mexico City), January–February 1981.
Phelps, Christi. "A Tale of Two Kings." *San Antonio Monthly*, April 1986.
Pisano, Marina. "The Kingdom Crowns Its Queens." *The Magazine of San Antonio*, March 1978.
———. "The Conservation Society." *San Antonio Magazine*, April 1979.
Remy, Caroline. "Hispanic-Mexican San Antonio." *Southwestern Historical Quarterly of the Texas State Historical Association*, April 1968.
Tolson, Mike. "What Eggs-actly Are Cascarones?" *San Antonio Light*, April 24, 1984.
Topperwein, Herman. "First Civil Settlement: Villa San Fernando de Bexar." *Texas Parade Magazine*, January 1973.
Young, Melanie. "Eight Decades of Fiesta Finery." *San Antonio Light*, April 28, 1985.

Other Sources

Battle of Flowers Association.
Files of San Antonio Conservation Society Newsletter.
Fiesta San Antonio Commission files and staff interviews.
Files of the *San Antonio Express/News*.
Files of the *San Antonio Light*.
University of Texas Institute of Texan Cultures at San Antonio.
Files of the *North San Antonio Times*.
Extensive interviews with many participants in past Fiestas.
Author's notes made when attending Fiesta events from 1936 to present.

Index

127